THE PARENT'S GUIDE TO

CHILDREN
WITH
TANTRUMS

**Practical and positive solutions for the
common problem of tantrums**

JONI LEVINE

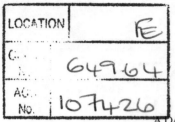
A DAVID & CHARLES BOOK
David & Charles is an F+W Publications Inc. company
4700 East Galbraith Road
Cincinnati, OH 45236

First UK edition published in 2006
First published in the USA by Adams Media, an F+W Publications Inc. company,
as The Everything® Parent's Guide to Tantrums in 2005

A catalogue record for this book is available from the British Library.

ISBN-13: 978-0-7153-2337-3 paperback
ISBN-10: 0-7153-2337-7 paperback

Printed and bound in England by
Antony Rowe Ltd, Chippenham, Wiltshire
for David & Charles
Brunel House   Newton Abbot   Devon

Visit our website at www.davidandcharles.co.uk

David & Charles books are available from all good bookshops; alternatively you can
contact our Orderline on 0870 9908222 or write to us at FREEPOST EX2 110, D&C
Direct, Newton Abbot, TQ12 4ZZ (no stamp required UK only); US customers call
800-289-0963 and Canadian customers call 800-840-5220.

tem′per tan′trum ▶n.

1. An uncontrolled outburst of emotion. Temper tantrums are sometimes referred to as fits or meltdowns and are a common behavior during childhood. Temper tantrums may include verbal outbursts, physical outbursts, or both.

Acknowledgments

I would like to express my appreciation to the many people who helped me or supported me during this project.

First, a special note of thanks for my steadfast proofreader, Beth Crowley, and content reviewer Helen South.

I am grateful for the many child development experts and child care providers who provided valuable anecdotes, resources, and feedback. Thank you Debbie Trouth, Sharon Drake, Sheila Milnes, Mattie Kendrick, Michelle Kindall, Susan Smith, Janiece Reid, Sandy Pelligrine, Tanya Albright, Jean Herbison, Eileen Donahue Brittain, Ellen Kay Closs, Penny Melby, Janet Irwin, Sharon Lillo, Ruth Archambault, Maria Goddard, Jill Berkman, Ann Luscan, and all the ladies on the Delphi Forums.

Special thanks to my cheerleaders! Maurice Wimbish, Thespine Kouvalakis, Viola Jones, T. A. Wyner, my dear parents, Barry Levine, and Sonja Bridgwood. Additional thanks to my editor, Kate Burgo, and my agent, Barb Doyen.

• • •

Contents

Introduction

Good news: Temper tantrums are normal! Every parent can expect to encounter at least a few meltdowns as their child grows. Although temper tantrums are often frustrating and upsetting behaviors to deal with, temper tantrums are as common as skinned knees, muddy shoes, lost game pieces, bogeyman fears, and all of the other day-to-day challenges of raising a child.

More good news: Your child's temper tantrums are not your fault! You have not caused your child to have temper tantrums, and it is not a reflection of your parenting ability. Even the children of child development experts have temper tantrums.

There is a lot of information about temper tantrums available. Unfortunately, that information is often very narrow and simplistic. This is the information that you will be likely to hear from TV, books, and even well-meaning friends and family. There are only three possible responses that are commonly mentioned: give in, punish, or ignore. The popular notion these days is that all children are motivated to have temper tantrums just for attention. If only it were that simple. The truth is that there are many possible reasons for your child's temper tantrums. Your child is a complex, unique individual and her behavior cannot be explained by a one-size-fits-all, cookie-cutter approach. You will find that this book will help you understand your child better. You will learn a lot about

the way that your child sees the world, the way that he feels, and what makes him tick. After all, you must understand your child's behavior before you set out to change it.

Give in, punish, or ignore? There must be more! And there is. The ideas and suggestions in this book go way beyond a quick fix. Yes, you will find specific real-life strategies for responding and coping with your child's temper tantrums and emotional outbursts. In addition, you will discover how to promote your child's emotional maturity and self-control.

Each time you respond to your child's temper tantrum, you have an incredible opportunity. You can learn how to handle your child's temper tantrums so that you can help your child to develop self-control. At some point, it will not be practical or possible for you to police your child in an attempt to guide or control his every move. If you use the strategies that you learn in this book, you will teach your child skills to independently manage her strong emotions of frustration and anger in the future.

This book will be your guide as your child grows. You will read about the common causes for temper tantrums for each stage of your child's development. You will find coping strategies that are appropriate and relevant, based on the cause of your child's temper tantrum.

You will also find advice on preventing temper tantrums, how to manage temper tantrums in special situations (at day care, while on a plane), and when to be concerned about your child's behavior. You will also discover simple and fun activities that you can use with your child that will not only help diminish temper tantrums but will also teach him social, emotional, and cognitive skills that he will use for a lifetime!

CHAPTER 1

Understanding Temper Tantrums

U nderstanding what a temper tantrum is and what causes it is half the battle in dealing with it. You must understand your child's behavior before you can try to change it. These emotional outbursts can be difficult to deal with and usually occur when you are least able to deal patiently with them. In this chapter, you will learn about what you can expect from your child's behavior throughout different age groups and stages.

What Is a Temper Tantrum?

A temper tantrum is essentially an uncontrolled outburst of emotion. Temper tantrums are sometimes referred to as fits or meltdowns, and are a common behavior during childhood. Temper tantrums are especially common between the ages of two and four and are seen routinely in about 80 percent of all children. Temper tantrums may include verbal outbursts, physical outbursts, or both. Temper tantrum behavior will be different for every child. Additionally, you can expect to see your child's tantrum behavior evolve as she grows. Common behaviors include crying and screaming, kicking, pouting, and hitting. These outbursts are generally quite intense, but fortunately, they do not last long. In fact, most temper tantrums begin to subside within the first minute and rarely last longer than five or ten minutes.

Common Behaviors

Even if you have not witnessed a temper tantrum, you probably have a good idea of what one looks like. The way that each child behaves when she has a temper tantrum is as unique as she is. The truth is, there is not any typical or atypical temper tantrum behavior. Each child is different. Below, parents share with you some of their experiences with tantrums. None of these examples is unusual, and perhaps you will see a bit of your own child in them.

Younger Kids

There will be times when your toddler is so emotionally distraught that you will be unable to determine what has caused this latest meltdown. Here are some examples of toddler temper tantrums.

"When my son was about two years old, he was overtired and one night he just had a meltdown. I remember him running around the house crying and screaming. At one point he picked up one of those Rubbermaid step stools and whacked himself in the head with it!" Jamie B.

"When my daughter was about fifteen months, we went to one of the state parks in our area, and went swimming at the beach. When it was time to leave, my daughter had a major meltdown because she did not want to go. I would put her in the stroller, and she would climb out—undo the buckle and everything! I ended up carrying her to the car. She kept blocking me from buckling her in. Finally I got her in the car seat, and she was still crying and screaming. I drove most of the way home with her like that, until she just conked out and slept." Jill B.

"We went to a local mall, and we were in the toy store. My two-year-old daughter started throwing a fit about wanting something. My husband and I both told her no and that if she did not stop, we were leaving. She did not stop. My husband was not done shopping, so I got the joy of carrying her through the mall to the exit. She was kicking and screaming the entire time." Sharon D.

"One night, my son was so distraught because I left to go for a walk, that he waited by the front door for me. Well, my husband called me, as I had my cell phone, and told me that I had to come in the back door. Here my son had cried while he sat in the box we have for shoes at the front door and he eventually cried himself to sleep in the box!" Tanya.

Preschoolers

The preschooler now has some verbal skills for expressing his emotion, which sometimes makes things more challenging.

"My daughter's worst temper tantrums are now peaking at age four. Before now, she usually just got mad. I would set her in her room, and tell her to come out when she felt like she could calm down and talk about it. Now I take her to her room, shut the door, and she bangs on the door, throws things around, and yells, 'Let me out of here. Open the door? Aaarrrgggh!' and so on. Repeatedly. And 90 percent of the time, it lasts about five minutes straight, and I will go in to find her asleep. She will try to tell me 'grown-ups are supposed to let kids do what they want. If you make me go in my room, I will scream and cry because I am not happy.' Most of her fits are about not getting to watch TV. That is her one hot button at four. Before this age, it was about fights with her friends. Now she's doing really well with playing nicely and sharing." Michelle K.

"My four-year-old is bossy to all the kids and she is downright demanding to me. Her tantrums are wild. We are at battle every day. It is so tiring. A lot of times I want to just give in and let her have her way just so there isn't a constant fight. It seems that as soon as she has been turned down for one thing, she instantly thinks of the next thing that I will say no to. It makes me think she is intentionally looking for negative attention." Belle R.

"My daughter is three and no matter what I say to her or how I say it, she has to say no. She always puts up a fight, and when she does not get what she wants, she starts to shriek." Maria G.

Toddler Temper Tantrums

The toddler years are prime time for temper tantrums. Some parents report that their children began having temper tantrums as early as one year of age. However, tantrum behavior is not very common until the child is two years old. It is believed that as many as 20 percent of all two- and three-year-olds will have more than two temper tantrums a day.

Because your toddler does not possess much self-control, his temper tantrums are likely to be very intense. Once he becomes emotionally worked up, he may have a hard time calming down and regaining control. Children will have their own unique way of throwing a tantrum. You may see your toddler cry, hit, throw himself to the ground, screech, flail, or kick when he has a tantrum.

 Essential

Your toddler's temper tantrums are not planned or intentional. There are many reasons why your toddler may have a temper tantrum, but all of the reasons stem from either environmental factors such as overstimulation or fatigue or from the natural development of your child's cognitive, social, and emotional maturity.

Toddlers do not have temper tantrums out of spite! There are some common reasons for toddler temper tantrums.

Separation Anxiety

Although you may witness your child having a temper tantrum when you leave when she is as young as ten months of age, separation anxiety usually reaches its peak around age two and a half years. If your child has separation anxiety, she may be very clingy and may throw a tantrum whenever you try to leave her. Children with secure attachments do tend to have less difficulty with separation.

Egocentrism

When your child is egocentric, she will have a hard time seeing and understanding someone else's perspective, and will think the world revolves around her. This results in temper tantrums about possession and sharing. Being egocentric also makes it difficult for children to negotiate and resolve conflicts with others, because they can see only their own point of view.

Autonomy

During the second and third years of his life, your child may begin to engage you in power struggles and display negativity as he starts to assert his growing independence and identity.

Lack of Language Skills

Without language skills, your toddler has limited ways to express her strong emotions. Unable to verbalize her frustration, she is more likely to lash out physically or burst into tears. Aggressive behaviors usually will diminish once a child acquires adequate language skills to use for conflict resolution.

Preschool Temper Tantrums

Although it is likely that your child will have temper tantrums through the preschool years, you should notice a decrease in frequency from the toddler years. Only about 10 percent of preschoolers will have more than two temper tantrums a day.

By the time he's in preschool, your child has acquired some ability to use language and to recognize and manage his emotions. Therefore, the intensity of his temper tantrum behavior will diminish. However, your child is still prone to strong feelings of anger and frustration. When your preschooler has a temper tantrum, you may see him throw things, hold his breath, stomp, yell, or whine. Indeed, strong emotions can still play havoc with your preschool-aged child's self-control. Your preschooler may still have temper tantrums because of separation anxiety and egocentrism.

Lack of Patience

Your preschooler still does not understand time concepts. She will have a hard time being patient and delaying gratification. When she wants something, she wants it now! Learning impulse control and patience to wait is a skill that your child will need to work on throughout her preschool years.

Frustration

Your child is acquiring many new motor, social, and cognitive skills. He has a need to feel competent and successful and, therefore, he often experiences frustration trying to do as well as the "big kids." The more he tries to master new skills and adventures, the more times he's bound to experience some failure. Young children need to learn to persevere and resist frustration.

Need for Attention

If you have been quick to respond to her pleas for rule changes, toys, and so forth by giving in to her demands, your child may begin to intentionally engage in tantrum behavior solely for the purpose of getting attention or something else that she wants. Temper tantrums can be a method either of attention getting or of manipulation.

School-Age Temper Tantrums

By the time your child enters school, temper tantrums will be less frequent; however, the occasional tantrums your child does have will still be troubling. When your school-aged child has a temper tantrum, it is unlikely he will flail about on the ground kicking and screaming. Rather, he may become defiant, sulk, swear, or become aggressive or destructive.

Your school-aged child has acquired a level of emotional maturity that should help her delay gratification and tolerate frustration more easily. Her improved cognitive abilities mean that she's no longer egocentric, and that she has a rudimentary sense of right and wrong. However, there may be times when children this age still have difficulty managing their stronger feelings. They are most prone to having temper tantrums when there is a major change or stressful event in their life, such as a death in the family or the family's moving to a new town.

**Fact**

Generally, aggression, along with temper tantrum behavior, will decrease as your child matures. Instrumental aggression peaks at ages two and three and even intentional aggression usually declines by the age of eight.

There are some common reasons why your school-aged child may still have a temper tantrum. Your child may still resort to tantrum behavior if she has learned that this is an effective way to get what she wants. Manipulation temper tantrums may increase as your child ages. When your child enters school, her social relationships expand. Along with many newfound friends, your child may face struggles with teasing, social isolation, and peer pressure. As your school-ager becomes more competent and independent, you may see an increase in defiance and power struggles as she begins to question your wisdom and authority.

Fear as a Factor

One strong emotion that may become particularly troubling for both toddlers and preschoolers is fear. For some children, strong fears and anxieties may result in a temper tantrum. Again, temper tantrum behavior may be the way that they deal with this strong emotion. Extreme fear will evoke an instinctive fight-or-flight response in your child. When confronted with something that is scary, your child may try to run, or he may resort to screaming and kicking. He will do whatever he can to avoid what he fears.

 **_Fact_**

Because preschoolers do not yet have the cognitive skills to understand the difference between fact and fantasy, they will often become afraid of irrational or fictional things. Fears of the bogeyman, monsters, clowns, witches, and so forth are common during this time of your child's development.

Respond with Empathy

Respond to your child's fears with empathy and patience. Even her illogical fears feel very real to her. Avoid ridicule or punishment, as that will only serve to increase your child's anxiety. Allow your child to approach what she is frightened of at her own pace. You can help her cope with fear by reassuring her and giving her some control over the situation. You can do this by saying, "I promise that I will keep you safe at the circus. I know that the clowns frighten you. Where do you feel is a safe and comfortable place to sit?" After a while, you might say something like, "We have been sitting very far away from the clowns. We have seen that they are silly and friendly. Do you think that you are ready to move a little bit closer?"

Read All about It

You may also wish to share some of the many picture books about dealing with fears. Sharing a story is a safe way to talk about what is frightening for your child. Through the story, your child will be able to see how other children have learned to manage their fears. A good book to start with is _There's a Nightmare in My Closet_, by Mercer Mayer.

Take Action

Some parents discover that they can help their child conquer a fear by joining the child and taking imaginary action against the fear. This seems to work particularly well against fictional monsters, ghosts, bogeymen, and the like. Use a room deodorizer can to spray "monster repellent" in the closet. The fragrance can be tangible evidence. Go through the actions of locking the ghost up in a chest or box. Try asking your child to make a picture of what she is afraid of and then have her rip up the picture and throw it away or flush it down the toilet in a symbolic gesture. Assign a teddy bear or doll to stand watch over her if she is scared at night.

Alert!

Children learn through imitation. Your young toddler or preschooler will be aware of your fears and apprehensions. If they witness that you are afraid of something, they will be likely to be scared as well, even if they have never had direct exposure to what frightens you.

Temper Tantrum Myths

For most parents, parenting knowledge comes from two main sources: how they were raised and common knowledge gleaned from media and the advice of other well-meaning people. Some of this information will be useful, but at times, it may be based on outmoded views, different beliefs, and even faulty research. Not all of what you have heard about temper tantrums may be true.

Temper Tantrums Are Unhealthy

Wrong. Not only are temper tantrums normal, but also they serve a healthy purpose. For young children with limited language skills, these outbursts are often the only way to communicate their needs. In addition, temper tantrums provide your child with a much-needed outlet to vent their strong emotions of anger and frustration.

A Temper Tantrum–Prone Child Is a Bad Child

Wrong. Temper tantrums are not bad, and neither are the children who have them. Temper tantrums are not preplanned events. With rare exception, your child does not set out to willfully misbehave when he has a temper tantrum.

 Essential

You will surely receive a lot of advice on parenting and disciplining your child from well-meaning friends and family members. Some advice, indeed, will be valid and helpful. Just be sure to pick and choose what is appropriate for your individual child and situation.

Temper Tantrums Lead to Delinquency

There is no evidence to prove this. Most of your child's temper tantrums are a result of developmental issues. If you help your child acquire self-control as she learns appropriate ways to express her strong emotions, you should expect her to become a happy and well-adjusted teen and adult.

You Are a Bad Parent Because Your Child Has Temper Tantrums

Wrong. There are many reasons why your child may have temper tantrums, and none of them is a reflection of your ability to parent. Even the children of child development experts have temper tantrums.

There Is Nothing You Can Do about Your Child's Tantrums

If that were true, this book would not exist. Although you have not caused your child's temper tantrums, there are many ways that you can prevent them. In addition, you can help your child to acquire the skills to express himself in a more appropriate fashion.

All Temper Tantrums Are for Manipulation

Wrong. This may be the most widely propagated myth. Many parenting books, and even well-meaning friends and family, will tell you to ignore your child when she has a temper tantrum. In fact, this is valid only for attention tantrums, which occur with minimal frequency in children older than three or four.

Responding to Your Child's Tantrum Spoils Him

Wrong. For many temper tantrum situations, the most appropriate response is to respond with compassion and gently guide your child. This is particularly true for the frustration and emotional temper tantrums that are common for toddlers. When young children are out of control, they need you to patiently help them reestablish emotional control.

Alert!

Recent surveys show that 68 percent of parents still approve of spanking as an appropriate discipline technique. But research shows that spanking a child has been tied to an increase in reactive aggression and retaliation behaviors. Children who are spanked are more likely to lash out at other children who are aggressive toward them.

You Should Always Have Full Control over Your Child

Wrong. Helping your child gain control over his actions does not mean that you must have full control over him. You should not try to break a child's spirit or will. Your ultimate goal is to help him become independent and able to regulate his own behavior, not depend on you to police his every move.

There Is One Right Way to Cope with Temper Tantrums

Parenting is never a one-size-fits-all endeavor. There are many strategies for coping with your child's temper tantrums. What works for your child will be as unique as your child is. In fact, you are bound to discover that you need to be flexible, and as your child grows, you will need to adjust your response. You may even find that what worked last week does not work now. Flexibility is key.

CHAPTER 2

Temperament and Temper Tantrums

Y ou thought you had parenting down to a fine art. After all, raising your first child was a breeze. She was a happy-go-lucky and very calm baby. She was friendly and sunny and temper tantrums were few and far between. Now, your second child has come along and turned your understanding of parenting on its ear. You are sure you're doing exactly the same thing, but your second child seems so fussy and cranky all of the time. Even the slightest upsetting event will cause her to have a temper tantrum. Can it be true that some children are more prone to tantrums than others?

What Is Temperament?

Indeed, some children are more prone to temper tantrums than other children are. Psychologists believe this may be due to a child's temperament. Temperament is your child's inborn disposition. Your child's temperament is his characteristic way of responding and reacting to events and his environment. Your child's temperament will be fairly stable throughout his life, but it is not set in stone. His temperament will surely be influenced by interactions and experience as he matures.

In the now classic New York Longitudinal Study, researchers identified nine basic temperamental traits. The variance of how a child exhibits these traits determines the child's temperament type as difficult, easy, slow to warm up, or mixed. Although most parents are unfamiliar with the nine identified traits by name, they know their child's temperament. In fact, more parents will observe these traits very early on. By the time a child is four months old, her temperament is usually apparent.

Question?

Is my child's tantrum caused by temperament?
When questioning the cause of a temper tantrum, rule out the following considerations before blaming temperament: Is the tantrum developmentally related (e.g., lack of language skills)? Is your child ill or under a lot of stress? Does your child have a developmental or behavioral disorder?

Three Basic Temperaments

Psychologists have identified three main temperament types. It is important to note that each category or type may encompass a wide range of behaviors. Very few children will be a perfect match to any one type of temperament. However, you may find that a majority of his behaviors fit in one of the three types listed below.

The Easy Child

You will be able to tell early on whether your child has an easy temperament. She will be a calm and content baby. Not much will seem to upset her. Her behavior is reasonably predictable. Not many things seem to startle or upset her. Loud noises, new people, strange places—she adjusts well and takes it all in stride.

Slow to Warm Up

If your child has a slow to warm up temperament, he will not be as easygoing as the child with an easy temperament is. Children with this temperament are often cautious about new people or situations, often withdrawing first and taking a while before they feel comfortable. Additionally, it may take them longer to adjust to change.

As many as 35 percent of all children will not fit neatly into a type, possibly displaying behavior characteristics of all three types of temperament. Happily, close to 40 percent of all children can be classified as having an easy temperament. About 10 percent of children will have a slow to warm up temperament, and fewer than 15 percent of all children will consistently display characteristics attributed to a difficult temperament.

Difficult

The child with a difficult temperament is often a feisty, cranky, or fussy baby. She reacts strongly to new people or situations. She seems to be upset easily, and it is difficult for her to calm down.

Traits Associated with the Three Types of Temperament			
Trait	**Easy**	**Difficult**	**Slow to Warm Up**
Activity	low	high	low
Distractibility	low	high	moderate
Adaptability	good	poor	slow
Approach/Withdrawal	approach	withdrawal	initial withdrawal
Intensity	low	high	mixed/low
Regularity/Rhythm	regulated	unregulated	regulated
Sensory sensitivity	high	low	moderate
Mood	positive	negative	mixed
Persistance	low	high	moderate

Traits Weakly Associated with Tantrums

These temperament traits are part of the nine that are considered when determining a child's temperament type. These traits do have a weaker relationship to tantrum behavior, but they are a part of your child's total temperament and affect his behavior and disposition.

Distractibility

If your child has a high level of distractibility, he will have a hard time paying attention. When he is engaged in a task, his attention is easily diverted by external stimuli such as background noises. It may seem that he has a hard time following directions, or that he is not listening to you at all. The child with a difficult temperament is more likely to have a high level of distractibility.

Alert!

Some level of distractibility is normal for young children. The ability to focus comes with increased cognitive skills. Young children naturally have a short attention span. Sitting still for more than ten minutes can be quite a challenge for a young child.

Activity Level

The child with a difficult temperament often has a high activity level. You will be able to observe this when your child is still an infant. The infant with a high activity level is restless, fidgety, and squirms a lot. As she grows, you will notice that she always seems to be on the go. She hates to be confined or constrained. Getting her into the car seat may be a battle every time. Additionally, you may find her so active that she becomes wild or out of control.

Persistence

Persistence is a mainly positive trait. A child who is usually able to attend well to a task without giving up is a persistent child. If your child is persistent, he is more likely to be able to tolerate frustration. There is a downside to having a child with a high level of persistence. At times, he may become stubborn in his attempts at completing a task, even when it is not feasible. One mother relates, "My son refused to quit any task he started. If he was struggling to zip his jacket, he refused help. No matter that we may be running late; once he had a goal in mind, he would fight to accomplish it. If his dad or I stepped in, he would have a fit."

Regularity/Rhythm

This trait refers to the predictability of your child's patterns of sleep and hunger. Many infants will fall into a consistent sleep and hunger schedule at around four to eight weeks of age. If your child has low regularity, you will have difficulty getting her on a schedule. As she grows, bedtime conflicts may become common. Some nights you may find that she is cranky and falling asleep early, and other nights she may be wide awake, unable to settle down, and very resistant to bedtime.

Traits Strongly Associated with Tantrums

Some temperament traits are more strongly associated with temper tantrums. Low adaptability, low sensory threshold, low approachability, along with high intensity and a negative mood are traits more commonly seen in children with difficult temperaments. In many cases, you will be able to see a direct link between a trait and your child's troublesome behavior.

Adaptability

Many children with difficult temperaments have low adaptability. Adaptability is the ability to handle transition and change calmly. If your child has low adaptability, she becomes upset when there is a change in routine. She is unable to go with the flow. She may be very resistant to change. Anything unexpected easily throws her off balance.

Approach and Withdrawal

This trait refers to a child's response to new situations or people. Children with a difficult temperament are more likely to be cautious or anxious when meeting new people and may be clingy or shy in those circumstances. They are often resistant to trying new things, whether it be a new vegetable or a different brand of sneakers.

 Essential

Keep in mind that it's normal and fairly common for young children to experience some shyness. Even a child who is fairly outgoing may show some hesitation at first. The difference is, unlike a child with withdrawal, other children do not react strongly to all new situations, and their shyness will usually fade after ten to fifteen minutes.

Intensity

All children experience happiness and sadness. However, each child varies in the way he responds to his own emotions. For example, two children may win a prize at a carnival. One child smiles broadly and the other child jumps around shrieking and hollering. If your child has very intense reactions to emotion, he may have a more difficult temperament. The very intense child may react strongly to even the slightest displeasure, perhaps earning a reputation as a drama queen or king.

Sensory Threshold

Is your child very picky or fussy? She may have a low threshold for sensory stimulation if she responds strongly to mild stimulation from things such as noise, room temperature, pain, or odors. "Bath time was battle time," recalls one mom. "I could barely touch my daughter with the washcloth without her cringing. The water was always too hot or too cold. The soap was too slimy, and the shampoo stung her eyes. It was a nightmare."

Mood

This trait refers to the child's prevailing disposition. Even the most cheerful child will be in a bad mood on occasion. In contrast, the child with a negative mood trait seems chronically unhappy or dour. He has a more pessimistic and negative outlook on life.

Why Temperament Matters

It will be helpful for you to know your child's temperament. You will gain valuable insight into your child and her behavior. If a child with a difficult temperament is challenging you, you probably wish to get at the root of the problem. Some parents report wondering if their child is emotionally disturbed or has brain damage. Perhaps you found yourself viewing your child in a negative light by labeling her as a crybaby or a wild child.

A child with a difficult temperament is as normal as a child with an easy or slow to warm up temperament. Once you know and understand your child's temperament, you can view your child's behavior objectively. This will help you to refrain from emotionally lashing out or withdrawing from your child. Understanding your child's temperament will give you the insight to plan accordingly and avoid potential problems for your child. For example, if you know your child is slow to adapt, you can be sure to warn him in advance before bedtime.

Goodness of Fit

Although temperament is inborn, a child's experiences and environment do have an impact. "Goodness of fit" refers to a parenting approach that accounts for individual differences in your child's temperament. Effective parenting is not one-size-fits-all. Your parenting style has goodness of fit when your expectations and demands match your child's temperament. Goodness of fit will help you respond appropriately to your child's unique temperamental traits.

 **Fact**

> When your response to your child's temperament is not a good fit, you will have difficulty managing your child's temper tantrums. In addition, your child could experience stress if your expectations do not match his temperamental style.

It's important to be flexible and adjust your response to meet your child's temperament. You will find that there will be a higher probability for conflict if your own temperament varies greatly from your child's. If you are impatient, you may have a hard time holding back when your very persistent child insists on taking her time to complete a task. If you are outgoing in social situations, you may be displeased when your shy or withdrawn child does not approach your friends in a bold fashion.

Although much of goodness of fit relies on the way you respond to your child's specific temperamental traits, you can follow some basic guidelines: Do not try to change your child's temperament. Rather, show respect for your child's uniqueness. Avoid comparing your child to another child. Avoid statements like, "Why can't you sit still like your brother?" or "I never had a hard time spending the night away from home, and neither should you." Focus on the positive. Even traits associated with a difficult temperament can be positive. The intense child may also be creative. The slow to adapt child may be more analytical and methodical.

Responding to Traits

You will eliminate a lot of stress and conflict with your child if you respond appropriately to his temperament traits. You will have a goodness of fit if your expectations and reactions match your child's temperament. Being sensitive to your child's individuality allows you to adapt your responses to calm your child rather than make things worse.

Slow to Adapt

If your child is slow to adapt, he thrives on predictability and routine. You will find that change and transition are difficult for him. You can prevent many problems if you establish a daily routine. Try to keep events in your child's life as predictable as possible.

Prepare your child in advance when there will be a change. This is helpful whether the change is small (lunch will be late) or large (she's starting a new school). Take time to discuss with your child what will be happening and what she can expect. If there is to be a major change in your child's life, maintain as many of your child's routines as possible. For example, while on vacation in a hotel, try to maintain your child's normal bedtime routine.

 **Essential**

Probably the most difficult and common transition time for your child will be when you ask her to stop playing and clean up. This does not have to be a dreaded chore—you can make it fun. Try turning cleanup time into a game. Challenge your child to beat the clock. Perhaps you can pretend the toys are real and she is putting the dolls to bed, parking the cars, and so forth.

Every day of your child's life is filled with transitions: coming in from playing outside to get ready for dinner, taking a bath, and getting ready for bed. The slow to adapt child will have difficulty during these times. Often, your child will be deeply engaged in an activity and he will find it difficult to abruptly stop what he is doing. Give him a warning that he needs to end his activity soon. Be concrete and specific. Rather than saying, "We are leaving soon," try telling him,

"We will have to leave in five minutes, so you need to finish your project." Help him find closure by prompting, "What else do you wish to paint on the picture so that you feel it is finished?"

Approach/Withdrawal

Many children are hesitant or cautious in new situations. They may be reluctant to enter a theme park, hesitant to go with you to visit the neighbors, or withdrawn when meeting new people. After ten to fifteen minutes though, most children become more comfortable in a new situation.

If your child is having great difficulty and withdraws or excessively resists new situations, there are some ways you can put him at ease.

- **Show appreciation.** Everyone approaches new situations at his own speed. Let him know that this is okay.
- **Avoid labeling.** Labeling her as shy has a negative connotation, and you may create a self-fulfilling prophecy.
- **Go slow.** Encourage, but do not push your child to approach. Be sensitive to his level of comfort. If you push him, he is likely to feel anxious and he will resist more.
- **Avoid reinforcement.** If you make a fuss and coddle your child when she is reserved, she may learn to increase the behavior for attention.
- **Stay quiet.** Avoid speaking for your child. Speaking for him diminishes his need to approach people and speak for himself.
- **Make the challenge manageable.** Break it into small steps. If your child is not ready to play the musical chairs game with the other children, perhaps she can help play the music for a while.
- **Recognize triumphs.** Acknowledge when your child reaches out: "I am glad to see that you felt comfortable enough to say hello to Aunt Elise."

Mood

If your child has an overall negative mood and disposition, it is unlikely there is much you can do to change it. You can, however, help reduce her pessimism. Help her recognize the positive aspects of a situation. Take the time to point out the silver lining behind her gray cloud. For example, you could say, "Yes, the weather today is dreadful, but what a great day to pop some popcorn and watch a movie!" Encourage her to focus on the bright side by asking her questions like, "What was the funniest ride at the park?" or "What is something good that happened today?"

High Activity

There are two main strategies for coping with your highly active child. You can prevent problems, and you can give her appropriate outlets for her excess energy. Once you recognize this temperament trait in your child, you can anticipate situations that may be problematic for her. Recognize that sitting still and waiting will be particularly trying. Places like doctor's offices and restaurants are likely to be unpleasant places to take your active child. If it is not possible to avoid these types of places, plan ahead to reduce problems. Take along a diversionary activity for your child, such as a handheld game. While you are there, scout out opportunities for your child to get up and move. Choose restaurants with play areas or at least a buffet. When you are in a waiting room, sometimes even a brief walk up the corridor can be helpful.

Give your active child plenty of opportunities to burn off steam. Whenever possible, balance quiet activities with more active ones. One smart father found a way to make long car trips with his son manageable. He took the time to pull off the road for a break every hour. They got out of the car and did exercises such as running in place or jumping jacks. This father found that the time lost for these "pit stops" paid off with a calmer, more pleasant trip for everyone.

Distractible

It can be very frustrating if you feel that your child is never paying attention to you. When your child does listen, she often only completes half a task before wandering off, mentally, if not physically.

Multistep tasks are particularly difficult, as your child may become distracted midway through completing the task. Keep directions simple and break them down step by step. Instead of saying, "Go over to your dresser, get your blue socks out of the top drawer, fold them, and put them in your suitcase," try, "Go to your dresser. Okay—now that you are there, open your top drawer." Alternatively, you may find it helpful to prompt your child to keep him on task when he seems to get lost with multistep tasks: "Okay, you folded the socks, now where should you put them?"

Alert!

Make an effort to capture and hold your child's attention. Approach your child directly, rather than calling out from the other room. Use his name when speaking to him. Whenever possible, get down to his level and make eye contact.

Intensity

Children with difficult temperaments often respond to situations with a high level of intensity. Whereas a cut on the finger may cause one child to whine and ask for a Band-Aid, the intense child may scream as if she has been mortally wounded.

It is a natural response to mirror someone's behavior and emotions. In other words, when someone is whispering, you will be inclined to whisper, too. This is especially true when your angry child is screaming and crying. You may find that your automatic response is to yell and exhibit anger as well. This behavior will usually cause your child's intensity to escalate, so it is important that you stay calm.

A child with a high level of intensity will be the most inclined to lose emotional control. It will be helpful if you tune in to your child. Learn to recognize her signals that indicate a flare-up is approaching. This is the best time to intervene. Help your child become self-aware, too, as you attempt to squelch her outburst prematurely. "I can see that the puzzle is really starting to frustrate you. Why don't we go for a walk, and then we can work on the puzzle later, when you feel calm."

CHAPTER 3

Making It Worse: Internal Factors

Why is your child having so many temper tantrums? Sure, you may be looking at his temperament or possibly the influence of recent stressful events in the household. However, the solution to preventing many of your child's temper tantrums may be even closer. Learn how internal factors such as hunger, fatigue, and sensory stimulation can affect your child's behavior.

The Influence of Nutrition

Proper nutrition is crucial for your child's growth and health. What and when your child eats will affect his physical well-being as well as his behavior. Just like adults, hungry children are more likely to be irritable, aggressive, and easily upset.

When Kids Should Eat

Breakfast is the most important meal of the day. Research has proved that this well-known adage is true. Research studies have shown that when young children skip breakfast, they are more inattentive and sluggish throughout the day and perform poorly in school. Eating a nutritious breakfast also sets the stage for healthy eating throughout the day. Children who skipped breakfast were found to be more likely to crave sweets later in the day, therefore being more prone to experiencing a blood glucose roller coaster.

 **Question?**

What is a child-sized portion?
Obviously, children require smaller portions than adults do. Although each child is different, a good rule of thumb is to start with one table-spoon of a food for each year of your child's age. Let children know they can always ask for seconds if this is not enough.

The best way to prevent your child from being hungry and expe-riencing midday slumps and irritability is to provide him with small and frequent meals. Rather than serving your child the traditional three meals each day, divide the daily portions into five or six mini meals or snacks. While he's awake, attempt to have something to eat available for him every three or four hours. Not every meal needs to be of equal size. For example, you may serve a full breakfast and lunch and then provide smaller meals midday and in the evening. It is wise to maintain a set time schedule for meals and snacks. Of course, there will be times when you will have to veer from this, but try to stick to it when you can. Some experts recommend that you avoid giving your child food at any other time than a scheduled meal or snack. This is a good idea if your child's constant munching is spoiling their mealtime appetite.

There are ways that you can ensure a successful meal experi-ence in which your child is calm and eats well:

- Get your child to settle down a few minutes before mealtime. If you have her stop an activity to sit down and eat, she may be too restless. A brief story time will usually do the trick.
- Do your best to make mealtime calm and relaxing. No one eats well when she feels stressed or hurried. It may be helpful to serve all meals in the same location. Do not let your child roam around the house while she eats.

- Start by serving your child small portions so that you do not overwhelm her. She can always ask for more. Remember that you can decide how much food to serve your child, but you cannot decide how much she is going to eat.
- It is natural and acceptable for young children to play around a bit with their food. However, if they are only playing and not eating, or if they are misbehaving at the table, odds are that they are done and should be allowed to leave the table.

What Kids Should Eat

Proper eating is about more than the quantity and frequency of meals. What your child eats is just as important as when and how much he eats. A balanced and nutritious diet is essential. Researchers are learning that there are certain foods that will affect your child's behavior.

The controversy remains regarding how sugar in a child's diet influences his behavior. It has long been an accepted theory that consuming a lot of sugar or sweetened foods causes children to become hyperactive. Interestingly, there has never been scientific evidence to support this claim. However, it is known that a diet that is high in sugar and carbohydrates will play havoc with your child's blood glucose levels. Ingesting these foods will cause the blood glucose to rapidly rise and then fall sharply a short time later. When glucose levels drop low (hypoglycemia) your child may feel sluggish, irritable, and cranky.

 **Fact**

Vitamin B_6 is very important in your child's diet. This vitamin is used in making neurotransmitters that impact behavior. A deficiency in vitamin B_6 can indeed lead to your child's being hyperactive and impulsive. They may also experience sleep difficulties and be more aggressive and prone to temper tantrums.

Although sugar may not be directly at fault for your child's poor behavior, food additives and artificial coloring may very well be. Recent studies do show a link between food additives and artificial coloring and hyperactivity and temper tantrums. Some studies claim that as many as 25 percent of all temper tantrums may be caused by these substances.

There have been a few additives and colorings that have been directly identified to potentially impact your child's behavior. The most common ones are:

- Preservative—Sodium benzoate E211
- Artificial coloring—Tartrazine E102
- Artificial coloring—Sunset Yellow E110
- Artificial coloring—Carmoisin E122
- Artificial coloring—Ponceasu 4RE124

Eliminating these substances from your child's diet can be challenging. "My daughter's doctor told us to avoid all artificial flavors and colors," one father relates. "Halloween was a particularly frustrating time, as the only candy that fit the bill was Reese's Peanut Butter Cups. She had to give all of her other candy away." Take the time to read labels. Although there has been a heightened awareness about this issue and many companies are changing what they put in foods, you will still find artificial coloring in 41 percent of all fruit drinks, 23 percent of cereals, and as much as 78 percent of all store-bought desserts.

The Picky Eater

Your child's tastes and appetite, which may fluctuate wildly, will influence the size and frequency of her meals. As she approaches two or three years of age, her appetite may diminish somewhat. Your child's physical growth rate is slowing down and therefore her food needs are less. She may develop stronger food preferences and aversions that could also affect her appetite. Be aware that some children are sensitive to food textures—your child may be repelled by things that are too mushy or too crunchy. You are bound to see peaks and valleys on a daily basis in your child's appetite.

Almost all children go through a phase where they will be picky. Some children develop food jags, where they will insist on eating only certain foods. In this situation, you can take one of two approaches. First, if you are so inclined, you can try to cater to your child's wishes. This is tough unless you want to play short-order cook for your child all of the time. Alternatively, you can just continue to serve your child what you normally would and adopt the attitude, "If he is hungry, he will eat," which, in fact, is true.

Alert!

Be very careful of what foods you serve to children under the age of four, as they are more likely to choke than older children are. Avoid small round or cylindrical foods like nuts, popcorn, grapes, hotdogs, and hard candy.

It is best to approach your child's fussy eating with some flexibility and a sense of humor. Take heart, even if your child eats less for a few days, his nutritional intake over the course of a week will usually be adequate. As a general guide, the average toddler needs 1,000 to 1,300 calories a day.

There are some things that you can do to try to make foods more appetizing and appealing for your child. You can take the time to make the food more attractive by adding or changing the color. If he decides that orange food is icky, try mashing the baked squash with a bit of red food coloring. One creative mother had a child who would drink only chocolate milk (Mom was not happy about this), so when the child was not present, she added blue, red, and green food coloring until the milk was a muddy brown color! You can also make food more attractive with a simple garnish or decoration. Cheese toast always tastes better when it is cut into fancy shapes with cookie cutters. Foods that children can eat with their hands are always more appealing, for some reason. Do not give up hope of getting your child to eat vegetables other than French fries and ketchup. Some children who will refuse cooked vegetables are happy to eat them raw, cut up, and served with dip. If all else fails, you can disguise many vegetables within other foods that your child will eat, such as soups and stews. Contact your pediatrician if you witness dramatic or persistent changes in your child's appetite, at any time.

Teaching Kids How to Eat Right

From the start, you are responsible for feeding your child and providing adequate nutrition. You make careful choices about how and what to serve your child. You have the opportunity to lay a foundation for good eating habits both for now and for the future, when they start to make their own food choices. You are your child's first teacher, and kids learn by observing and imitating you. Healthy food choices should be the rule, not the exception, in your home. Be a good role model by making good food choices for yourself.

Healthy Choices

Offer a variety of foods. There are countless culinary choices available. Take advantage of these exciting choices as you try to meet your child's nutritional needs. Perhaps he does not care for oranges or orange juice. Why not try grapefruit, pineapple, or even carambola?

Reconsider the snack food that you have available for your child. Avoid sugary and carbohydrate-laden treats. Replace cookies, donuts, and candy. Try these nutritious snack ideas instead: sunflower seeds, yogurt, trail mix, dried fruit slices, celery with peanut butter and raisins (Ants on a Log), string cheese, cucumber and cream cheese sandwiches, or cottage cheese and fruit.

What your child drinks is also important. A recent survey found that, on a daily basis, as many as 35 percent of toddlers drink sweetened fruit drinks, and 10 percent of toddlers drink soda pop! These beverages are just empty calories and offer no nutritional value. Your child needs at least two glasses of milk (or soy substitute) each day. You should not serve reduced-fat milk to children younger than two years old. One hundred percent fruit juice is fine on occasion, but remember that whole fruit provides better nutrition. Water is also a good beverage choice for your child.

Alert!

When offering new foods to your young child, introduce only one new food at a time. Wait for four or five days to rule out an allergic reaction before introducing another new food.

Involve Your Child

Involve your child in food choice and preparation. While at the grocery store, point out the value of the food you are selecting. "Oh, I think I will get some of the broccoli for our dinner. Broccoli has many vitamins and minerals that will help our bones and teeth stay strong. Can you help me pick a large green bunch?" Allow your child to be a minichef in the kitchen. Even young children can help stir or mix, and you will be surprised how eager they will be to taste something that they helped prepare!

Encourage your child to try new foods. However, realize that forcing your child to eat something will just cause resentment and further resistance. Do not give up though. Some children will have to be exposed to a new food more than ten times before they will taste it.

Occasional treats are okay. A special treat of cookies and milk for a party, or a piece of pie at the holiday cookout, is fine. When you allow your child to indulge for a special occasion, she will come to view sweets as special treats for special occasions rather than as forbidden fruit or everyday fare.

The Influence of Sleep Deprivation

Sleep is a biological need, essential for survival. Not only does sleep give the body a chance to rest and heal, but it is necessary for healthy brain functioning as well. A good night's sleep regenerates and rejuvenates us, getting us ready to face the challenges of a new day with a fresh perspective. Ironically, a rested child falls asleep more easily than a child who is overtired does. Young infants will sleep whenever they need sleep. When they are tired, they will simply fall asleep, regardless of the time of day or the setting. However, by the time your child is nine months old, he will be able to stay awake even if he's tired. This may be due to noise, excitement, stress, or many other factors.

Is Your Child Getting Enough?

Young children, in particular, need regular and adequate sleep to maintain both their physical and emotional health. There is a long list of behaviors associated with inadequate sleep, including: decreased concentration, diminished attention span, increased irritability and restlessness, lowered energy and activity levels, problems with coordination, defensiveness, anxiety, and increased impatience. It is easy to see how many of these behaviors can be associated with an increased tendency for temper tantrums. Research shows that when preschoolers get less than the recommended amount of sleep in a twenty-four-hour period, the children are 25 percent more likely to display opposition, noncompliance, or aggressive behavior.

 Essential

You may be able to determine that your child is not getting enough sleep. Twenty-five percent of all children exhibit the classic signs, which include difficulty or resistance to waking up in the morning, becoming cranky or irritable in the afternoon, and complaining of being tired or falling asleep during activities.

How Much Does He Need?

Studies show that parents are underestimating their young child's need for sleep. In fact, it was discovered that as many as half of all infants are regularly getting one or two hours less sleep than they truly need. The table that follows is a summary from the National Sleep Foundation's study. It compares the amount of recommended sleep for a child to averages of how much sleep children are actually getting. It is important to note that the duration and regularity of the sleep-wake cycle is what determines a quality and restful sleep.

Recommended Sleep Times versus Actual Sleep Times		
Age	Recommended Amount of Sleep	Actual Sleep
Infants	14–15 hours	12.7 hours
Toddlers	12–14 hours	11.7 hours
Preschoolers	11–13 hours	10.4 hours
School-age	10–11 hours	9.5 hours

The Power of Naps

Naps are an important part of your young child's sleep regimen. A restful nap will often stabilize your child's mood, revitalize her energy level, and ward off a great deal of her irritability and crankiness. Although each child's needs are different, there are some general guidelines you may wish to follow. A nap period is most beneficial when it is at least ninety minutes long. Many children under the age of two will require two naps each day, one midmorning and another one shortly after lunch. A majority of preschool children will still need the afternoon nap. The length of the nap may range between one and a half and three hours and may vary depending on your child's needs.

Use your own judgment when determining that your child no longer needs to nap during the day. Most five- and six-year-olds will be able to go smoothly through the day without a nap. However, it is still advisable to schedule a quiet, restful time as part of your child's afternoon. Perhaps a set time for reading or quiet table games.

What Keeps Your Child Awake?

Sometimes a good night's sleep can be an elusive goal. There are many things that may interfere with your child's rest, diminishing how much sleep she gets. However, there are concrete ways to combat these factors and help your child establish lifelong healthy sleep habits in the process.

Most people will wake up several times during the night. Often these are brief occurrences, say to change position or adjust a pillow, and are forgotten by morning. Your child, however, may wake up fully and have difficulty falling back to sleep. Reasons why your child may wake in the middle of the night include bad dreams, illness, environmental noise, and dry air that causes a stuffy nose, making it difficult to breathe.

Bed-wetting

Bed-wetting (enuresis) is common in children through the age of five. Some children will wake up as soon as they soil their bed, while others will continue to sleep soundly. Bed-wetting is not an intentional behavior, so don't make a big fuss about it. Punishing or ridiculing your child only adds shame and fear when he is probably already embarrassed about wetting his bed.

You can try to help your child stay dry through the night. Limit his intake of fluids in the evening and ask him to use the toilet right before he goes to sleep. Some parents find it worthwhile to rouse their child at set intervals during the night to see if the child needs to use the bathroom. Most likely, your child will outgrow bed-wetting. Bed-wetting in older children may be caused by stress, small bladder capacity, or even genes. (Yes, it can be hereditary!) Do not hesitate to contact your child's pediatrician if you are concerned.

Nightmares and Night Terrors

Nightmares and night terrors can be particularly troublesome. Night terrors are usually experienced by only young children. The peak is between ages three and five. Nightmares can occur at any age but are more prevalent in children than in adults.

Night terrors are more frightening for you than they are for your child. Your child does not fully wake up during a night terror and will not remember it in the morning. If your child is having a night terror, she may scream or cry. She will usually seem to be partially awake and exhibit extreme fear or agitation. She will be very hard to calm and will often not recognize or respond to you. Night terrors are not harmful. The best that you can do is maintain a calm demeanor and keep your child from acting out in response to the unknown terror. Because night terrors occur while your child is in a phase of deep sleep, they are most likely to occur during the first half of the night.

Alert!

During the preschool years, your child's nightmares may star fantasy and fictional creatures such as bogeymen, witches, and monsters. Preschoolers do not have the cognitive maturity to fully understand the difference between fact and fantasy, so these images may be particularly distressing for them.

Toward morning, your child spends more time in light sleep. This is when both dreams and nightmares occur most frequently. When your child awakens from a nightmare, he will usually be understandably frightened and often disorientated or confused. Your best course of action is to be sympathetic and comfort your child. He may need a lot of reassurance that the nightmare was not real and that he is safe, before he can fall back to sleep.

Fear of the Dark

A fear of the dark is very common in young children. As with other fears, you need to be sympathetic toward your child. There are a few ways that you may be able to make your child more comfortable. Try playing soft music to calm and distract your child. Help your child get used to the dark. Take a walk around the neighborhood or a familiar place when it is dark. As your child becomes more comfortable, you can play a game of hide-and-seek in the dark with flashlights. There is nothing wrong with allowing your child to have a nightlight. The soft glow of a colored bulb or the light from a fish tank will also usually do the trick.

Getting Kids to Bed

Parents often report that bedtime is a leading source of conflict between themselves and their child. You know that a good night's rest is essential for your child's emotional calm the next day, yet bedtime itself seems to spark many temper tantrums. Bedtime is often trying for both you and your child, as you are both probably tired to begin with and your coping skills have worn thin. Fortunately, there are specific things that you can do to make bedtime a peaceful time.

Bedtime Routines

Set a routine. Bedtimes will be more pleasant for all if you establish a bedtime/evening routine and stick to it. Consistency is key. Of course, special events may occasionally disrupt your plans, but follow the set schedule whenever possible.

A set bedtime schedule will help your child feel secure, as she can predict and prepare for each step in the schedule. Also, an effective schedule or routine will be designed to help your child progressively wind down after her active day so that she will be ready to rest. Do not think you can wear out a child with play and such just before bedtime—this will just tend to gear her up when you want her to wind down. You may wish to include calming activities such as a warm bath and a bedtime story in your child's bedtime routine.

Essential

If you are having a difficult time getting your child to settle down at night, consider the beverages he is drinking during the day. Studies show that 26 percent of children older than age three drink at least one caffeinated beverage each day. Eliminate the soda pop from your child's diet for a more restful night.

Set the Stage

Your child's bedroom should be a quiet and restful place. You may wish to remove anything that will keep your child from sleeping. Many children now have a television or computer in their room. Research has found that children lose an average of twenty minutes of sleep each night when they have a television in their bedroom.

There are other ways that you can create a restful and calming bedroom environment:

- Make sure that the room is well ventilated.
- Adjust the room's temperature so that it is neither too hot nor too cold.
- Cut down on outside light by installing drapes or blinds.
- Add carpeting and drapes to cut down on outside noise.
- Consider running a fan or playing a CD of white noise to drown out outside noise.

Off to Bed

Set all bedtime routines and rituals in advance. Be clear with your child exactly what is expected of him. You may need to specify exactly how many drinks of water he can have or when he is permitted to get back out of bed. You could also let him read or listen to music while he is trying to fall asleep. Remember, although you can make your child go to bed, you cannot make your child go to sleep.

Unless you are allowing your child to share your bed, consider how you will respond if your child wakes and cries for you in the middle of the night. There are many different viewpoints on this; you must choose what is right for both you and your child. Some parents will choose to ignore the child, letting her cry. Other parents will respond immediately to comfort the child any way they can. Perhaps the most comfortable and effective approach is this: Respond to your child by checking on her. Reassure her verbally but avoid picking her up or making too much fuss. Stay firm that she needs to remain in bed and go back to sleep. You can then slowly increase your response time each night to break your child's dependence on you to get back to sleep.

The Influence of Sensory Overload

How your child responds and reacts to her physical environment and external stimuli can influence her behavior. Almost all children will have some sensitivity to sensory stimulation that can result in behavioral problems. Some children will exhibit the temperament trait of low sensory threshold, discussed in Chapter 2. These children will be overreactive to smells, sights, and/or sounds. They may respond as if they are being literally bombarded with too much stimulation. You will sometimes witness them avoiding and withdrawing by observable behaviors such as holding their ears or closing their eyes when they are overwhelmed.

Some children who have great difficulty in high stimulation situations, who exhibit great anxiety or distress, are found to have a sensory integration disorder (SID). This disorder can negatively impact learning, development, and behavior. A child with SID has insufficient neurological processing of sensory information. She may be over- or undersensitive to different types of sensory information and may often misinterpret mild sensory signals as producing great discomfort. It is possible that your child will have minor difficulty with some sensory systems without having SID. These difficulties, however, will surely influence her behavior.

 **Fact**

> Sensory integration disorder focuses on three sensory systems, which are complexly interconnected. These sensory systems guide how the child experiences, interprets, and responds to stimuli in his environment.

The Tactile System

One father describes his daughter who was oversensitive to touch: "For the most part, my daughter was a very affectionate child. She loved bear hugs and roughhousing. But when I tried to gently stroke her hair or pat her arm, she would shriek and jerk away as if I had burned her!"

If a child with SID has difficulty with her tactile system, she may be either over- or undersensitive to light touch, pressure, pain, or temperature. The oversensitive child will withdraw from or overreact to tactile stimulation. She may refuse to get her hands dirty or may even resist certain textured foods. The child who is undersensitive to tactile stimulation may crave touch or not be aware of painful stimuli.

If your child is oversensitive to tactile stimulation, there are specific things that you can do to make life more pleasant for both of you.

- **Choose clothing fabric carefully.** One hundred percent cotton is usually the best bet. Other fabrics may be scratchy or irritating. To this child, wool can feel more like steel wool.
- **Choose clothing styles carefully.** Sewn-in tags on the collar can be particularly irritating. Remove them whenever possible. Look for loose-fitting clothing that does not have bulky seams that can rub or irritate your child's skin.

- **Avoid accessories.** As a general rule, scarves, hats, jewelry, and dangling hair ribbons will be irritating to a child who is overreactive to tactile stimulation.
- **Experiment with grooming products.** Avoid shampoos and soaps with harsh additives or dyes. If toothpaste is unpleasant, try a gel. If a washcloth hurts, try a soft sponge.

Vestibular System

The vestibular system involves your child's inner ear and affects his sense of balance and his ability to detect his own movement. If your child is oversensitive to vestibular stimulation, he will complain of feeling unstable on his feet. He may be fearful of swings, slides, steps, or ramps. He may need reassurance and may often need to hold a railing or your hand to feel steady. The child who is undersensitive to vestibular stimulation will purposely seek out stimulating movement activities such as whirling or spinning.

Proprioceptive System

The proprioceptive system refers to your child's awareness of her body and its location in space. The child who has difficulty with her proprioceptive system may exhibit problems with depth perception and will be generally poorly coordinated and clumsy. The overly clumsy child may improve with practice with motor activities. Be patient with him and avoiding teasing him.

CHAPTER 4

General Guidelines for Coping with Temper Tantrums

The temper tantrums you witness are likely to be as unique as your child is. As she grows, why and how she throws temper tantrums are sure to change. You will find that how you respond to them may change depending on her age and development. However, you will find that there are some helpful general guidelines for responding to and guiding your child.

Your Emotional Response

When your child is in the throes of a temper tantrum and she is kicking and screaming, you are likely to have an emotional reaction. It is helpful to remember that many, if not all, parents have a hard time coping with their child's temper tantrums from time to time. You may experience any of the following emotions when your child is having a temper tantrum: embarrassment, aggravation, helplessness, guilt, and anger. All of these feelings are normal. It is also normal to doubt your own parenting ability at times like these. When your child is having frequent emotional meltdowns, you may be asking, "Am I spoiling her too much? Why can't I prevent this?"

Understanding Your Response

How you feel when your child has a temper tantrum is likely to vary each time. Sometimes, you may find yourself very agitated with your child's behavior and other times you may feel calm and patient. Your feelings

and responses will be influenced by how you perceive your child's motivation for his behavior. If you assume your child's motivation is negative (spite or attention), you will be more likely to feel angry or agitated. Consider, do you automatically think the worst? You may be able to change how you feel and subsequently respond. Avoid blame, and focus on the facts. Rather than attributing motivation to the behavior ("She is trying to push my buttons"), think about what is actually taking place ("She is crying when I tell her to put away her toys").

 Essential

When your child is in the throes of a temper tantrum, he may verbally lash out at you. Hearing your child announce, "I hate you!" may hurt you or anger you. Resist the temptation to respond emotionally. Recognize that your child is emotionally out of control, and he does not mean what he is saying.

When You Are Angry

Most parents occasionally report feeling angry when their child has a temper tantrum. If you respond to your child with anger or extreme emotion, you are likely to only fuel the fire. Your child's emotional response will often mirror your own. If you begin yelling or crying, you cannot effectively help to calm your child. Someone in the situation needs to be in control.

Examine your emotional response to your child's temper tantrums. You may be able to identify what triggers your impatience or anger. If there are specific situations that are trying for you, maybe you can find a way to avoid them. For example, bath time always becomes battle time. You are tired from a long day at work, and you just want to get your child into bed so you can relax. Perhaps you can ask your spouse to take over bath time, or you can move bath time to an earlier time in the evening when you are not so tired.

There still may be times when you will feel angry that your child is having a temper tantrum. Take a deep breath. Try the well-known technique of slowly counting to ten. If you are still too angry or upset, take a step back from the situation. You can set a good example for your child on how to manage anger. Say something like, "I am feeling very angry about your behavior. I need to sit down and calm myself." If your child is very young or is in danger of hurting himself, be sure that another adult can step in while you step back from the situation.

Your Parenting Style

There are many reasons why your child has temper tantrums. Some of those reasons are internal factors such as your child's temperament, his verbal ability, his cognitive maturity, or even his level of hunger or fatigue. Some reasons are external situations, including stress, loud noises, separation, and loss. Very rarely will you personally be the direct cause of your child's tantrum. However, the way that you respond to your child's misbehavior and temper tantrums can either reduce or increase the likelihood of problems.

 **Fact**

Studies show that there are some specific parenting practices that are associated with more aggressive behavior in children. Some of these practices include: poor supervision, a low involvement in the child's interests and activities, and harsh or erratic discipline.

Psychologist Diana Baumrind has identified three basic parenting styles. Each style looks at the balance of control in the parent–child relationship and its influence on the child's behavior and development. It is important to note that you will probably not fit exclusively into one category. Although you may find most of your responses fitting into one category, your parenting style may vary. Your mood, the circumstances, and even the birth order of your child may influence your parenting style.

To find out what your parenting style is, choose the answer that best describes your response or views regarding the questions below.

1. Your child starts to whine and cry because he doesn't want to take a bath. You
   (a) Give up, and try again tomorrow.
   (b) Ignore your child's protest. You will remove his clothes yourself if you have to.
   (c) Question him on why he is upset and then find a way to reassure him.

2. Your child asks to stay up late to watch a special TV show. You say
   (a) "That is up to you, if you think you won't be tired in the morning."
   (b) "Absolutely not! Your bedtime is always at 8:00, you know that."
   (c) "Why don't you tell me why the show is worth staying up for and I will consider it."

3. When it comes to setting limits for your child, you generally believe
   (a) Children should learn to set their own rules. Freedom will help them learn.
   (b) Your rules are the law. What you say goes.
   (c) Rules are important guidelines for behavior, but there may be exceptions.

4. Your child forgot to feed his goldfish again. You
   (a) Feed the goldfish.
   (b) Punish your child by finding a new home for the goldfish.
   (c) Ask your child what will help him remember to feed the goldfish. Perhaps a sticky note on his door?

5. Your child is refusing to sleep in her own bed. You
   (a) Let her sleep where she wants.
   (b) Admonish her for not being in bed after her bedtime.
   (c) Talk to her about things that might make her feel more comfortable sleeping in her own bed.

Permissive parents will answer mainly A. Authoritarian parents choose answer B the most. Authoritative parents are most inclined to select C. What are these types?

Permissive Parenting Style

The permissive parent gives most of the control to the child. She fails to set reasonable limits and often does not consistently enforce the limits that she has established. Permissive parents often allow the child to make decisions, and they count on their children to regulate their own behavior. Children of permissive parents are often uncertain or anxious about whether they are behaving appropriately. They are less likely to take risks or try new things. Additionally, children of permissive parents tend to develop less self-control.

Question?

What influences your parenting style?
There are many factors that will influence your style and approach to parenting. How you were raised will play a part, as well as whether you choose to reject or follow the style your parents used. Your own temperament, values, and beliefs about how children should behave will also impact your style.

Authoritarian Parenting Style

Authoritarian parents insist that they have full control. They expect their child to behave with unquestioning obedience. The children of authoritarian parents do not have a voice, and they make very few choices. The child is expected to fully conform and comply with all expectations without question. These children are more prone to temper tantrums. They are also more likely to be more withdrawn and distrustful than other children are. Children of authoritarian parents are also the most likely to exhibit rebellious behavior when they get older.

Authoritative Parenting Style

Authoritative parents share control with their children. Although they remain the authority, they encourage and respect their child's opinions and input. The child's voice is heard and her preferences are taken into account during decision making. Authoritative parents set consistent, reasonable, and firm standards of behavior. The child with authoritative parents is the most likely to be secure and self-reliant and to exhibit the most self-control.

Consider Your Child's Age

Temper tantrums are a normal part of your child's development. As your child grows, you will find that your child will have temper tantrums for different reasons. Additionally, there are different guidelines and strategies for each age group.

Toddlers

Toddlerhood is the peak time for temper tantrums. Common causes for toddler temper tantrums include: separation anxiety, an inability to understand another's point of view, a desire for autonomy, and immature verbal skills. Almost all toddler tantrums are the result of developmental issues. Toddlers do not intentionally engage in tantrum behavior for revenge or to get attention. They are socially, emotionally, and intellectually incapable of that thought process.

Allow your toddler's temper tantrum to run its course. Your young child needs an avenue for expressing and venting frustration, anger, and other strong emotions. Do not view your acceptance of your child's temper tantrums as being permissive. You are not coddling or spoiling her. Just be sure that you are not rewarding her with extra attention or praise for having a tantrum. The message you want to convey is, "I understand that you have strong feelings to work out. I am going to help you find more appropriate ways to express those feelings."

Alert!

Because they tend to lose both physical and emotional control, toddlers are the most likely to injure themselves during a tantrum. You need to stay calm and keep close to your toddler during a temper tantrum. You may even find that you will need to manage her safety by moving things out of her way, or holding her safely.

Your young toddler has not yet developed emotional control. Therefore, he may be frightened and overwhelmed by both his strong feelings and his loss of control. Many toddlers can be calmed down by being held. This may help them feel a sense of security and external control. Each child is different, though. Some distraught toddlers will find that being held is too restrictive and agitating.

Your toddler has a short attention span. You may be able to diffuse many of her temper tantrums by simply distracting her or redirecting her attention. When she is yelling for a candy bar at the store, you may be able to get away with a diversionary tactic like, "Look! I wonder what those balloons are for. Let's go see!" (Of course, this particular tactic is only okay if it is all right for your toddler to have a balloon.) When she is insisting on cutting her baby doll's hair, you might be able to redirect her interest to cutting paper scraps instead.

Preschoolers
Your preschooler should be having fewer temper tantrums than he did as a toddler. Common causes of tantrums for preschoolers include difficulty sharing, impatience, and frustration. Although many

of your preschooler's temper tantrums may be caused by immaturity, you may now begin to see your child use tantrum behavior as a form of manipulation to get what he wants or to get attention. You will find information on how to handle an attention-seeking tantrum in Chapter 12.

Your preschooler has many skills that can help her manage and express her emotions without having temper tantrums. You may simply need to guide her to use these skills. She is now less egocentric. She is learning how to see someone else's perspective, and she is developing empathy. When she is having a conflict with another child, you can simply ask her, "How do you think Carly feels when you push her?" If she is not able to answer this question, or is not yet ready to empathize, model by answering how you would feel in this situation. Be sure to capitalize on her improved verbal skills; encourage her to use words when she is angry or upset.

Older Children

Older children are typically more tolerant of frustration, and they have developed some self-control. You may still see your older child have an occasional temper tantrum. Although he has new abilities, he also faces new challenges. Some common causes for temper tantrums in your older child may include: difficulty in delaying gratification, frustration in tackling new physical skills or academic challenges, social rejection, and a desire for independence.

Your older child is more rational and logical. You should be able to reason and negotiate with him. Your focus here is not to control or manage your child's behavior. Instead, you need to help him develop the skills he needs to manage his own emotions and behavior. You can help your child to cope with his strong emotions as well as develop self-calming techniques and problem-solving skills. Chapter 18 will show you how to teach your child these skills.

Tracking the Cause of the Tantrum

The more you understand your child's temper tantrums, the better equipped you will be to cope with them. If you are able to identify what triggers a tantrum, you will have a better chance of preventing it. Keep track of your child's temper tantrums over a period of time—two or three weeks should be sufficient. It is wise to include input from any adults who interact with your child. They may be able to provide a fresh perspective. Be sure to include details on what happens so you will be able to recall the incident clearly.

It is worthwhile to keep a written diary or journal. A written journal will help you reflect back on your child's behavior. You will be able to look for patterns so that you can avoid conditions and situations that you discover are problematic. A written journal will also help you to be realistic and objective. Keep track of when tantrums happen, where, who is around, signs that led up to the tantrum, how your child reacted, and what it took to calm him down.

Sample Journal Entry	
Variable	**Comments**
Day of week	Tuesday
Time of day	Late afternoon
Who	It was just me
Warning signs	He was whining for a cookie about 20 minutes earlier.
Place	In front of the shoe store
What happened	He suddenly threw himself on the ground. Through his sobs, I heard him say, "No, I don't wanna go to the store."
Conclusion	I moved him over to a bench. I told him that I needed him to use words so I could help him. Finally, he was able to tell me he was hungry.
Comments	I think maybe hunger and fatigue got the best of him today.

After you've tracked her tantrums for a few days or weeks, look closely at the entries to try to discern a pattern. Are your child's temper tantrums occurring more often on certain days? If so, can you identify why that day may be problematic? Perhaps Mondays are particularly hectic, or Friday is the day when Aunt Sue comes to visit.

Are your child's temper tantrums occurring more at a certain time of the day? Maybe you will discover that your child is prone to temper tantrums when she is cranky in the morning, or right before dinner when she is getting hungry.

Who was present when your child had a temper tantrum? Do certain people seem to agitate your child? Is your child more likely to experience a separation tantrum with you? Is he more prone to stage a tantrum for attention when he is visiting Grandma?

 Essential

You may also wish to record how your child's temper tantrum was resolved. Was your child able to regain control independently? How did you respond to his behavior? Reviewing this information from a selected period of time may help you gain a better understanding of what is effective and what is not for coping with your child's tantrums.

Did your child exhibit any warning signs that he was about to lose control? If you can pinpoint the precursors to your child's temper tantrum, you may be able to begin intervening before things get out of hand. Early signs that your child is heading toward a tantrum may include one or many of the following: irritability, increased crankiness, sudden resistance to physical affection, and whining.

Is your child showing a tendency to have more tantrums in certain places? You may find that certain places are too stressful or stimulating for your child, and you may wish to avoid those places for a while.

Positive Communication Strategies

When you respond to your child's temper tantrums, what you say can have a big impact. When you talk to your child, you have the opportunity to calm her down and help her learn safe behavior and self-control. Positive communication will promote these goals. Additionally, when you use positive communication, you can boost her self-esteem and confidence. When you use positive communication to respond to your child's temper tantrums, you are focusing on the behavior, not the child. You are saying, "I accept you, but I do not accept your behavior."

Positive Statements

Your goal is to help your child learn safe behavior and self-control. It is important that you are clear when stating your expectations of your child's behavior. Most young children are given negative directions such as, "Stop that!" or "Don't do that!" When you tell your child, "Don't throw sand," there is no guidance or direction given. What should the child do? By changing your response to, "Keep the sand in the sandbox," you change the focus from a correction of her behavior to an instruction about what she should do. Your child may be readily able to conform to your expected behavior, and he will be more likely to do so independently. When you use the positive statement technique, "Don't run over there" becomes "Please walk on the sidewalk." "Stop coloring on the walls" becomes "Use your crayons for coloring only on paper."

"I" messages

"I" messages are automatically positive statements that state or define your expectations. They are usually met with less defensiveness and resistance and can be a powerful tool in communication. Notice the difference in tone between these two sentences:

"Why are you such a slob? Can't you ever clean your room?"
"I would like for you to pick up the toys and clothes off the floor."

Which of these is more likely to result in your child's compliance? Effective "I" messages can start with "I need," "I want," "I wish," and so forth. When you are using an "I" message, "You are too loud" becomes "I need for you to use an indoor voice." "It is mean to tease the cat" becomes "I want you to pet the cat gently."

Fact

"I" messages can be a very effective way to establish positive communication with anyone of any age. Encourage your child to also use this technique. When your child uses an "I" message, he is intentionally and clearly stating his needs. This is a big improvement from when he used tantrum behaviors to communicate.

Reflective Listening

Reflective listening is particularly helpful with children who are experiencing strong feelings, and for children who cannot have their desires met. The reflective listening technique has two parts. In the first part of the statement, you reflect or rephrase what you see or hear in your child's behavior. Like a mirror, you reflect her feelings back to her. The second part is your statement of contradiction or reality. For example, "I can see you are very angry right now, but I need you to put the blocks away," or "I know you want to see over the fence, but it is not safe for you to stand up there."

Negative Responses

Your positive responses can help your child calm down and cope with temper tantrums. However, negative responses and statements will ultimately sabotage your efforts. It is easy to fall into a pattern of using these responses. These negative responses are ones to avoid, as they will often lower your child's self esteem, confidence, and trust, which are needed for your child to develop self-control.

Threats

You may have threatened your child, "If you do not settle down, I am going to leave you here." There is a difference between warnings and threats. When you warn your child, you are stating the certain consequences to his behavior. Try saying something like, "If you don't settle down, we are going to go outside until you regain control." By contrast, when you threaten your child, you are mentioning a consequence you have no intention of using. These stated consequences are usually exaggerated and intended to intimidate or frighten your child; they often include abandonment, imprisonment, and physical harm.

Guilt

"I am going to have to miss my meeting because you are acting up." When you attempt to blame your child or make her feel ashamed, you are using guilt. If you make your child feel guilty, she is likely to doubt her own competence and worth. She may feel that she will never measure up. Children who feel guilty are usually less autonomous and confident. Additionally, your child may also begin using blame to account for his own behavior. When your child blames others for his behavior, he fails to take personal responsibility for his own actions and choices.

Alert!

Some guilt-inducing statements inadvertently give power to your child. When you say, "Now look what you have made me do!" or "It is your fault that I scream so much," you are telling your child that she has the ability to affect your mood or behavior. Avoid this, or your child may begin manipulating you.

Name Calling

"Stop screaming! You are such a brat!" Calling your child "lazy," "evil," "stupid," "sloppy," or "wild" is not an effective way to respond to her behavior. She will take these labels to heart. This often leads to a self-fulfilling prophecy, where she internalizes and meets those negative expectations.

Comparison

"Why can't you behave like your sister Anna does?" When you compare one child with another, you sow the seeds of resentment and bitterness between them. Again, comparisons can also damage your child's self-esteem. The only appropriate way to compare is if you compare your child with herself, by noticing how she has changed or grown. For example, "Wow, your manners have really improved since the last time we went to eat at a restaurant."

CHAPTER 5

Rewards and Punishments

The root of a temper tantrum is the loss of self-control. When your child is young, you have the ability to help him learn self-control and safe, appropriate behavior. How you respond to misbehavior, whether you choose to use punishment, rewards, or discipline techniques, will influence your child's ability to maintain self-control later on.

Your Responses Affect Your Child's Behavior

Every behavior has a result. At a very young age, children begin learning how their behavior leads to a result. When they toss their spoon on the floor, it makes a noise. When they cry, Mom comes and comforts them. These results (also called consequences or reinforcement) can be either positive or negative.

A positive consequence to a behavior increases the likelihood that your child will repeat the behavior in the hope of achieving the desired result. For example, if you praise your child for sitting still at the movie, she will be more likely to sit still the next time—because she wants to receive the praise. Conversely, a negative result will increase the likelihood that your child will stop a behavior to avoid the negative consequence. If you take away a favorite toy when she does not put it in her toy box, she will be more likely to pick up the other toys to avoid losing any more. By choosing your response carefully, you can shape your child's behavior.

Essential

> Because young children are just learning the principles of cause and effect, and their memory is not long, consequences need to occur soon after the behavior. The famous threat "just wait until we get home" has little impact on a young child, who will not associate a later punishment with his behavior four hours earlier at the mall.

Studies show that positive consequences are more motivating and influential on behavior than negative consequences are. Children will be more motivated to do something for a reward than they will be to avoid a punishment. It is worthwhile to use positive consequences when your child is behaving in a desirable manner. And you should avoid responding with positive consequences if your child is misbehaving. This seems logical but you may find you are doing just that. Suppose your child is interrupting you while you are on the telephone, so you give her a cookie to occupy her. Your child is having a tantrum and kicking the seat in front of him at the movies, so you put him on your lap. Remember that some children may sometimes view even negative attention (lecturing, yelling) as a positive consequence. This is particularly true for children who feel like negative attention is better than no attention. Consider carefully what is reinforcing to your child before you respond. You can read more about how children learn to have temper tantrums in this fashion in Chapter 12.

Many children learn to engage in some behaviors just for the attention or reaction it brings. These behaviors include whining, tattling, and swearing. Imagine a young child who uses a swear word without understanding its meaning. He sees his parents react with shock, receives a lecture, and quickly learns that he can bring a halt to adult conversation and divert attention to himself by using this word. Quite a lot of power for a child! But if parents instead react calmly to the child's use of a swear word, it doesn't create the same reinforcement. Say to your child, "That word hurts people's feelings. If you wish to speak with me, use polite words." Then ignore further swearing. Your child has no incentive to use the word to get attention, because you don't make a fuss.

Using Praise

One type of positive reinforcement you may choose to use to shape your child's behavior is praise. You can help your child understand your expectations and then have her conform to them. When you praise your child, you recognize the times your child behaves the way you wish, and you are encouraging her to continue to repeat the behavior.

Praise can be very reinforcing and motivational to your child. Praise may also help boost your child's self-esteem. Praise communicates your approval and acceptance of her behavior. The more she is concerned with your opinion, the more your praise will influence her behavior.

However, you must use praise sparingly. Your child's self-image can become closely tied to your praise. If he comes to expect it frequently, he may be hurt when you do not praise him. Some children can become dependent on praise and dependent on someone's evaluating their every move. Just like flattery, praise loses its impact when it is overused. Your child will probably not attach much value to your recognition of a major accomplishment if he's used to hearing lavish praise all the time. For example, "Wow, look how nice you are sitting at the table. Great job using your fork. Oh my! I am so proud of you for eating a carrot!" Your child will not be as motivated when you say, "You did a wonderful job writing your English essay."

Essential

Do not forget that there are other positive ways to acknowledge your child's efforts or accomplishments. Sometimes simple gestures will do the trick. Try these: a wink, a high five, a broad smile, a hug, or a pat on the back.

Praise is most effective if you make it clear which behavior you are acknowledging. You are showing approval of the child's behavior, not their character. You may also choose to praise specific accomplishments or effort. Praise phrases such as "Way to go" or "Good job" are often not specific enough to influence your child's behavior and encourage him to repeat the desired behavior. Here are some examples of specific and clear praise:

- "I am glad that you remembered to say 'please.'"
- "Good work in waiting for your turn."
- "I really like how you shared your blocks with your sister."
- "Super! I am pleased that you helped Mom with the dishes."
- "You worked so hard on your science project, and it shows."

Using Treats and Tokens

In the long run, positive discipline techniques will be the most effective in helping your child learn safe behavior or self-control. There may be times, though, that you wish to react or respond immediately to a specific behavior or habit that your child has adopted.

When your child is exhibiting a behavior you do not like and wish to discourage, your first step is to identify and address the cause or issue. Many temper tantrums are caused by specific triggers you can reduce. When your child is in control and making a clear choice with her behavior, you may wish to try a token or treat system of reinforcement. Treats and tokens work best if your child is older than five years old. Younger children have a hard time delaying gratification. Each time your child behaves as you wish or completes a specified task, you reward him with a token (poker chip, coin) or a mark (check mark, sticker) on a visual chart. He is then able to redeem the token or marks for a prize. These systems can be particularly effective for children because they are concrete and visual ways to measure or track success.

Set Up a System

Keep things simple. Be very specific regarding what behavior you are targeting. Avoid vague goals like "behave in the store" or "play nice." Rather, clearly define specific behavioral expectations: "Stay seated in the cart" or "Share your toy with your friend." Define exactly what she needs to do, when she needs to do it, and how well she needs to do it. For example, "Every time that we go to the grocery store, you must stay seated in the cart's seat. You must keep your bottom on the seat and not stand up until I remove you."

Limit the period of the reward system. As soon as your child begins to master the behavior consistently, you need to phase out the program so she does not rely solely on the reward. Three or four weeks is usually sufficient.

How Will You Reward?

If you use tokens, what item will you use? How will they be collected or stored? For charts, will you use check marks, stars? Will you recognize different levels of compliance? For example, you may choose to have blue chips if your child completed the task independently. Red chips may be used if you had to remind him once. You could use white chips if you had to ask him directly more than once.

For younger children though, it is best to keep it simple and just have just one level.

When can he redeem his rewards for a prize? Every day? Once a week? You may wish to have small and larger prizes available. This way, he can choose to redeem one or two chips/stickers at the end of the day for a small prize or save some to earn a larger reward at the end of the week.

You do not have to be extravagant. Simple tokens or prizes often work well. Be sure to choose something that is age appropriate and of interest to your child. Here are some possible rewards:

- Mini deck of cards
- Super ball
- Coloring book
- Pack of gum
- Hair ribbons
- Trading cards
- Puzzle book
- Mini action figures
- Stickers
- Spinning top
- Silly sunglasses

Alert!

Avoid using food as a reward. Experts agree that using food as a reward or punishment sends the wrong messages. From this practice, unhealthy attitudes and habits about food could emerge.

When Will You Give a Reward?

You may choose to give a chip/sticker each time the child behaves as you wish. You may also wish to reward after a set time. For example, "If you say 'please' at least once today, at bedtime I will put a star on the chart." Remember, the younger your child, the sooner he needs recognition or reinforcement. After your child starts to comply on a consistent basis, you may wish to stagger the reinforcement schedule. Instead of giving your child a sticker every time he shares a toy, give him a sticker every third time he shares a toy. After another few days, you can increase the interval time until your child is no longer expecting or depending on the reward to be motivated.

You may choose to put priority on which behaviors you will reward. After all, it is not practical to reward every good deed and kind word. Alternatively, you may taper off the frequency with which you use rewards. As you do this, you can focus your child's attention on possible intrinsic rewards: "Look how happy you made Tony feel. Doesn't it feel good to help out a friend?"

Use rewards sparingly. If you rely on them constantly, your child will come to expect them. Eventually your child will be behaving as you wish because she is motivated by the reward. Her intrinsic (internal) motivation will diminish. She won't behave appropriately for self-motivating reasons such as self-worth or altruism. If this happens, once the rewards stop, so will the desired behavior. No longer will she cheerfully volunteer to help you carry groceries or help her little sister with homework because she enjoys being helpful and kind. Each time she behaves positively, she will be wondering, "What is in it for me?"

Punishment versus Discipline

If you are like most parents, you view discipline and punishment as interchangeable approaches to guiding your child's behavior. In fact, they are very different. Each one has a unique set of goals, techniques, and outcomes. Often your role in discipline is that of a teacher guiding your child and teaching him safe behavior and self-control. When you punish your child, your role is more likely like that of a police officer, trying to keep your child in line and obedient.

Because it directly teaches appropriate behavior and teaches skills, discipline is more effective than punishment for handling your child's unwanted behavior. Additionally, recognizing and reinforcing positive behavior is more influential in changing your child's behavior. Besides having differing goals and strategies, punishment and discipline affect the child in different ways. Punishment often humiliates, degrades, angers, embarrasses, or discourages. Discipline often builds self-esteem, shows respect, models coping skills, and encourages.

What Is Discipline?

Discipline is largely a positive, proactive approach. The main goal of discipline is for your child to learn safe behavior and self-control. Ultimately, discipline helps your child to regulate her own behavior so that she is able to make independent choices and decisions. Positive discipline can teach children many things, such as:

- How to delay gratification
- How to develop a system of values and morals to guide them
- How to behave appropriately in a variety of settings
- How to follow societal and cultural standards of behavior
- How to use conflict resolution when relating with other people
- How to predict consequences of their behavior
- How to control and express their emotions appropriately

The techniques discussed below will help your child to go beyond behaving just for a reward or praise or to avoid punishment. These strategies will help him develop an intrinsic motivation and inner control for behaving appropriately.

Redirection

Redirection is a powerful discipline technique for younger children. You guide the child to change his behavior to be safer and/or more appropriate. When you witness your child misbehaving, help him change either the action or the victim (person or object).

Redirecting Behavior		
Original Behavior	**Change of Action**	**Change of Target**
Cutting doll's hair	Brush doll's hair	Cut paper
Coloring on the table	Wipe table	Color on paper
Feeding Play-Doh to pet fish	Feed fish food to fish	Feed Play-Doh to pretend fish

Redirection works best when you guide the child gently, explaining why the change is needed. For example, "Jumping on the bed is not safe. If you feel like jumping, let's go outside and do jumping jacks" or "Jumping on the bed is not safe. Beds are for resting, so if you want to be on the bed, you need to lie down."

Consequences

You will not always be there to guide your child's actions. She needs to learn the consequences of her behavior. If you use consequences, you will help your child learn to think before acting and will teach her to take responsibility for her decisions. The main message to this technique is "Let the result fit the action."

Natural consequences are also known as life experiences or "the school of hard knocks." You do not choose a response to your child's behavior; there is a natural result: If she skips breakfast, she will be hungry later. If she breaks a toy, she will no longer have that toy to play with. There are times when it is not appropriate to allow your child to experience natural consequences. If the consequences are in any way harmful for your child (such as drinking a poisonous chemical or cutting himself with a knife), you must stop the behavior and use a different discipline technique, such as redirection.

Logical consequences occur when your response imitates real life. If your child colors on the wall, then he must help wipe it off. If your teen does not put his socks in the laundry, then he will have to wash the socks himself or wear dirty socks. It is helpful that you impose logical consequences that ask for your child to repair or "make good" on his misbehavior.

Time-out

Time-out is a technique that has gained popularity recently. It can be an effective tool, but it is often overused. It is best not to use time-out for offenses when redirection or even a simple discussion will do. Reserve the technique as a time and place for the child to step back and get control. When your child is hurting others, a time-out may be necessary to separate her from the other children so she can regain control.

Fact

A young child's attention span is very short. For time-out to be effective, it should occur right when you intervene, as soon as the child misbehaves. Most experts recommend that you limit the time your child spends in time-out to one minute for every year of his age. So, for example, a four-year-old would spend a maximum of four minutes in time-out.

Be sure to explain to your child why you are putting her into time-out. You may say something like, "You are out of control and could hurt the baby. I am going to have you come away from him and sit in time-out. You need to calm down so you can play safely." Choose an area for time-out that is easy for you to supervise. Also, try to have time-out in a location that is not overstimulating or rewarding. You may not want to use the child's bedroom. She may start to view this as a negative place and be reluctant to go there when you wish her to, such as at bedtime.

What Is Punishment?

The main goal of punishment is to stop a child from misbehaving at the moment. Most parents also punish their child in the hopes that they will deter the child from repeating the behavior. Whereas discipline is often proactive, punishment is often simply reactive. You react to the child as you see her misbehave.

Keep in mind there are some times that your child may find punishment reinforcing. This is particularly true for children who are craving attention. To them, negative attention is better than no attention at all. If you yell and carry on when your child is having a temper tantrum, you may unintentionally be giving him what he wanted, and therefore he will repeat the behavior.

Types of Punishment

There are three main types of punishment: consequential punishments, verbal punishments, and physical punishments. Consequential punishment is different from the positive discipline techniques of logical and natural consequences. When a child misbehaves, there are still direct results of a behavior that occur, but unlike the discipline techniques, consequential punishment does not directly relate to the behavior. When you use a consequential punishment, you remove privileges or possessions that are valuable to your child. For example, "If you do not stop screaming at your sister, you can't go to the zoo" or "No TV if you don't clean your room." It is important to note that younger children truly have a hard time understanding the cause-and-effect relationship. Even older children often view this punishment as unfair or arbitrary, and it rarely produces long-term results.

Verbal punishment includes threatening, yelling, belittling, or embarrassing. Calmly explaining the reasons for a rule and discussing possible solutions for misbehavior is not punishment. Physical punishment is rarely effective and includes spanking, pinching, slapping, and shaking.

Why Not Spanking?

Spanking is a physical form of punishment. It is not a type of discipline, as it does not teach safe behavior or self-control. It sends a message that hitting is an appropriate way to respond when you are displeased or angry with someone.

 **Fact**

Physical punishment takes a toll on your child's emotional development and well-being. Studies show that regularly spanking a child results in their developing a chronic anxiety or fear of being hit. They are also more likely to develop a sense of helplessness and diminished self-esteem.

Spanking your child when he is being aggressive is about as logical as screaming at him when he forgets to use a quiet voice. Spanking a child sends a mixed message: "Hitting is not acceptable unless you are bigger or angry." Children who are spanked, even infrequently, are more likely to become angry and then even more aggressive. They may show this anger in retaliation against you. Additionally, they may displace their anger toward an innocent target such as a younger sibling or perhaps the family dog.

Punishment, whether consequential, verbal, or physical, may stop your child from misbehaving at that given moment. However, punishment does very little to prevent temper tantrums or misbehavior, as it does not teach your child skills for safe behavior or self-control.

CHAPTER 6

Don't Go: Separation Tantrums

Y ou have left your nineteen-month-old daughter with Grandma before. In fact, your mother has been a regular babysitter since your daughter was born. But now, out of a clear blue sky, your baby is behaving as if Grandma were a stranger by screaming and clinging to you for dear life. She used to cheerfully wave good-bye and now she has an iron grip on you. Why this sudden change in behavior? Will you ever be able to get out the door?

How Do Young Children Become Attached?

Your child will experience anxiety when separated from someone only if he has an established attachment with that person. Psychologist John Bowlby identified attachment as a lasting psychological connection between human beings. It is important to note that attachment is not an event but an ongoing process that peaks at approximately six or seven months of age. It is not, as was once believed, a "now or never" occurrence that happens at birth. It is also not limited to a birth mother and child, but instead is a process that can involve anyone who serves as the young child's primary caregiver. Therefore, separation anxiety can occur with anyone the child has formed an attachment to. A secure attachment protects a child from harm and fear and assists the child in eventually becoming an independent and confident adult.

How Attachment Starts

Many mothers report feelings of love and attachment long before the child is even born. The awareness of these feelings comes at different times for different people. Perhaps you felt a bond the first time you felt your little one kick. Or when you saw the sonogram. Or heard the heartbeat. Maybe you were instantly in love the moment you knew you were pregnant. Maybe you didn't feel that connection until you held your child in your arms. All the same, sharing your body with a child for nine months is a powerful way to start a relationship.

Your newborn is ready to start a relationship with you. Contrary to past belief, it is now known that a new infant is much more than an unaware, unresponsive being. In fact, your child has many tools to help her be a social human and enter relationships from the very beginning of her life.

Your newborn's sensory capabilities are amazing! Her sense of hearing is fully developed at birth. Your child has been able to hear in the womb for the last trimester of your pregnancy. Your newborn will often show recognition to specific melodies or voices that are familiar. Overall, newborns show a preference for the human voice and respond the most to a higher-pitched voice, especially their mom's.

 **Question?**

What is motherese?
Motherese is a universal style of speech that adults unconsciously adopt when they are speaking to infants. Someone who is speaking motherese talks in a high-pitched voice. She speaks slowly and uses repetition and exaggerated sound.

Your newborn has other preferences as well. Early on, he will show recognition and preference for his mother's body odor and even the smell of her milk. At birth your baby's vision is not fully developed. Newborns are nearsighted, with the optimum focal range of eight to ten inches. What is remarkable about this, is that this range matches the distance between your eyes and your baby's eyes when you hold him in a feeding position, allowing for intimate eye contact. Other studies show that very young infants show a preference for looking at actual faces rather than at photos or patterns.

Social interaction may begin right after birth. Although newborns spend most of their time sleeping, most will be in a "quiet alert" stage immediately after birth and will remain so anywhere from a half hour to three hours. This is an optimal time for the first step in the process of loving attachment.

Alert!

Illness of mother or child, use of various medications, and adoption are just a few reasons why bonding time immediately after birth may not happen. However, it is not a cause for alarm. Studies show that attachment will develop when the primary caregiver is nurturing, consistent, and responsive, regardless of when the bonding process begins.

The Building Blocks of Attachment

During your child's first year, the process of attachment strengthens. Your interactions with your child are key. You are laying the groundwork for a future relationship. Early on your baby will develop an interest in you. Without you noticing she will move in rhythm to your voice, mirror your emotional disposition, and mimic your facial expressions.

Early Interaction

Psychologist Erik Erikson identified the first two years of life as the time during which your child develops trust. The outcome of this stage impacts future development. A child who develops mistrust in infancy will become a generally wary and suspicious person.

Children who do not have their needs met consistently will learn that they cannot count on other people. They will be inclined to view the world as an unpredictable and hostile place. If the opposite happens, the child will be generally more open and optimistic. Children who develop trust and secure attachments have caregivers who are very responsive. Being a responsive parent means being in tune with your child and picking up on her cues. It means being aware of her body language and learning to decode her cries.

 Essential

In a famous experiment, Harry Harlow showed that bonding was based on more than just having physical needs met. He placed baby monkeys with substitute (surrogate) mothers. Some surrogate mothers were made of wire and wood and others were covered with soft terry cloth. The baby monkeys became attached to the cloth monkeys, using the wire surrogates only for food. When it comes to bonding, physical intimacy can be just as important as food.

Your infant is completely dependent on you for his very survival. Your child is learning whether he can count on you. Can he rely on you to feed him when he is hungry or cover him when he is cold? Although it is not practical or expected for you to hover over your child and react quickly to every anticipated need, consistency in attending to his needs is important.

Emotional Bonding

Remember that your child has emotional needs as well as physical needs. She relies on you for attention, affection, and comfort. The myth that attending to a crying infant will spoil her has long been dispelled. Especially in her first six months, none of your child's cries are arbitrary or purposeless. You will quickly learn what each of your child's cries signifies. Whether your child is crying because she is hungry, tired, or in pain, each cry is an attempt to communicate her needs to you. Consistently responding results in less crying and dependence later on.

Physical Bonding

Physical proximity also strengthens attachment. Many child development experts advocate carrying your child close to your body. Carrying your child close allows him to hear your heartbeat and voice and feel constant touch. Some say having your baby close simulates the pressure, motion, warmth, and security he experienced in the womb. Additionally, when your child is close, you are able to stay in tune with his distress cues and respond promptly. Studies show children who spend a greater time close to their mothers' bodies early on are less likely to be clingy and dependent.

 **Fact**

Parents in Asian cultures generally keep their young infants closer to their bodies. Two-thirds of the time, American infants are separate from their mothers. They are in cribs, swings, strollers, et cetera. In contrast, Korean parents hold their babies as much as 90 percent of the time. In Japan the family bed is a common practice until children reach adolescence.

Causes of Separation Anxiety and Tantrums

It might seem logical to believe that a strong attachment would result in your child's having more difficulty with separation. Surprisingly, the opposite is true. A securely attached child develops an inner confidence and security that allows him to boldly enter the world as an individual and develop new relationships. He learns he can count on you for reassurance and security. In fact, children who were securely attached infants are more likely to be outgoing and they initiate interactions with others easier.

Essential

In the long run, attachment types can impact future personality traits. A securely attached infant is more likely to be a child who is well adjusted, trusting, secure, and confident. An insecurely attached infant is more likely to be a child who is clingy and who craves attention or approval. An ambivalent or anxiously attached infant is more likely to be lonely, insecure, or withdrawn.

There are three main types of attachment. As described above, if you develop a trusting and secure bond with your child, she will become securely attached. Securely attached children cry when Mom leaves but are happy when Mom returns. They comfortably use their mother as a secure base for exploring the world around them. They do not fear abandonment or rejection.

If Mom has rejected the child's attempts to seek comfort and reassurance from her in the past, the child is more likely to become insecurely attached. Insecurely attached children often don't cry when Mom leaves but they also avoid reunions when Mom returns. The insecurely attached child may pull away when Mom attempts to pick him up.

If Mom's past response to her child's needs has been inconsistent, the child may become ambivalently or anxiously attached. The ambivalently or anxiously attached child will often show anxiety before Mom begins to leave and be the most clingy and upset during separation. The child's reaction upon reunion is inconsistent and sometimes anxious.

Evolving Emotional and Cognitive Abilities

Your child is more likely to experience separation anxiety as he matures. Even negative behaviors can indicate positive gains in your child's development. Both new cognitive and emotional abilities may increase the likelihood your child will experience difficulty with separation.

Object Permanence

One cognitive ability is called object permanence, or the ability to understand that something still exists even when it's not part of your child's environment or current experience. It is believed that, in the first few months of life, an infant's reality is limited to what is in her immediate consciousness. If she cannot see something, it simply does not exist. In other words, it's "out of sight, out of mind."

This limited perception is true regarding people as well as objects. Although your infant may show clear recognition and joy when she sees you, when you are away, you are not part of her immediate reality. Your infant is not lying in her crib wondering, "Now, where did Mom go this time?" or "I wonder when Daddy will return to feed me."

Question?

How can I tell if my child has object permanence?
Gently remove a toy your child is playing with and place it underneath a visible blanket. If your child shows no reaction to the toy's absence, she does not have object permanence. As she begins to grasp this concept, she will first show some reaction to the missing toy. If she has object permanence, she will actively look for the missing toy.

Most children will start to develop object permanence at approximately seven to nine months of age. When they finally have the cognitive ability to know you still exist when you leave the room, they may begin to experience separation anxiety.

Emerging Emotional Abilities

Your young child is gaining many new emotional skills. The process of attachment between you and your child is growing stronger and reaches its peak around seven to ten months. Your child is also becoming more and more aware of his surroundings. You may notice an increase in his interest in both his environment and other people around the time he is beginning to sit up. At first your child is likely to exhibit this newfound interest in others in a positive way. Many children will grab at a stranger's face, pulling their hair or poking at their mouth. They are actively learning about others and comparing them to Mom.

Somewhere around seven to nine months of age, your child will reach the realization that the person is indeed not Mom. It is then that you may see your child become anxious around strangers. In fact, some children may become anxious around those very familiar to them, including a favorite aunt or sibling. For some children, only Mom will do!

One mother shares, "My mother babysat for Jamie at least twice a week. Jamie loved Grandma. Jamie would coo and giggle whenever I handed her over to my mother. Then, almost overnight, this all changed. Jamie would scream and cry when I would try to pass her to my mother. She would become so hysterical, you would think that I was asking an alien monster to hold my daughter. The hysterics would continue until I was out of sight for at least ten minutes. My mother was so hurt by this; she thought she had a close bond with Jamie."

There are additional factors that will determine your child's reaction to separation.

- **Temperament.** Some children cope better than others do to new or strange people and situations.
- **Stress.** If your child is under stress or there are a lot of changes in his life, you may see more problems with separation anxiety.
- **Fear.** Consider the circumstances. Even a child who is securely attached and has no history of separation anxiety may have a hard time spending the night somewhere new or being left with a doctor in an exam room—any place that may cause them to be fearful.
- **Experience.** The more positive experiences with separation your child has, the more likely it is she will handle it well. She will see that she can predict and rely on Mom's behavior. She

will see that, indeed, Mom will return when she says she will. Most children will outgrow separation anxiety by the age of three or four. This is when they fully understand that Mom will return for them and, more importantly, that she is there for them emotionally even when she is not there physically.

Alert!

Each child's progress though developmental milestones will differ and so will their sensitivity to the dawning of stranger anxiety and/or separation anxiety. It is important to realize that both of these may begin at approximately the same time in your child's development. Your child may or may not react strongly to one or both. Leaving your child with a babysitter at this time may indeed be a double whammy.

Paving the Way for Smoother Good-byes

Even if your child is securely attached, has an easy temperament and experience with separation, he may experience anxiety from time to time. The process of learning to separate from you is a gradual one, but there are ways you can make separation easier, by being sensitive to his feelings and preparing him in advance whenever possible.

Practicing Separation

Around the age of ten months to one year, your child will be practicing many new physical skills. This is also a time when she will begin practicing separation. You will see this as your child becomes bolder when strangers are around. She may begin to spend less time on your lap or clinging to your legs. Your child will slowly explore around herself, often returning to you for comfort or reassurance. Your child will use you as a secure "home base" as he ventures further away and maybe even begins to approach new people. For example, your new neighbor is visiting. When your toddler enters the room, he immediately runs and hides behind your chair. After a few moments, he peeks out and then hides again. A few minutes later, he comes out and climbs onto your lap. Eventually he climbs down and sits by your feet and plays with your shoes. When the neighbor laughs loudly, he seems startled and gets back on your lap. When your neighbor smiles at him, he gets off your lap again. This time he retrieves a toy from a shelf and offers it to the neighbor. This time of practicing will often last through toddlerhood, and the process is not always a smooth one.

Get Ready for Separation

It is important to prepare your child in advance before separation events. Give her the opportunity to understand and process the idea. Take this time also to address any specific concerns she may have. Take care to convey a positive attitude. Sell the idea as much as you can. Instead of "I am sorry, Mommy has to go out and leave you with a babysitter, please don't get too upset," try "Mommy will be going out for a bit this afternoon. While I am gone, you get to play fun games with the babysitter!"

Keep your promises. Here is a chance to establish trust with your child. Be clear on what she can expect. Don't promise your child you won't leave, when you will, or that you will come home at a certain time unless you are sure you will be there. If you promise your child that you will return at lunchtime and you are indeed there, your child will learn that she can let you go and feel confident you will return as promised.

Transitional Objects

Your child is learning that you are a stable and constant source of love, comfort, and reassurance, even when you are not physically present. Until your child reaches this point, a transitional object is often helpful. A transitional object is an item that is comforting and soothing for a child as it often represents a tie to you or the security you represent. Transitional objects may take many forms, including blankets ("blankies"), a teddy bear, or even an article of clothing.

Essential

Photographs can be used as transitional objects with great success. Let your child have a photo of you to have when you are separated. This will help provide a concrete reminder of your presence, especially if it's a photo of you and your child together.

Responding to the Tantrum

Despite your best efforts to prevent separation anxiety, it still is likely there will be times you will contend with a crying and clinging child as you walk out the door. Separating from your young child may be just as stressful and heart-wrenching for you as it is for her. Be aware that your child will pick up on your apprehension and may feed off your negative emotions; if your body language is rigid and your voice sounds stern, it's not going to have a good effect. Resist negativity or implications that this should be an upsetting time. Some parents find that they are hurt when their child fails to show separation anxiety and tend to suggest directly or indirectly to the child that he should be upset. If your child is calm or unaffected by your preparation to leave, a statement like, "I know saying good-bye is scary, but don't cry" can be just the trigger to upset him—which is what you're trying to prevent in the first place.

The Mad Dash

If your child demonstrates true difficulty in saying good-bye, you may consider taking the easy way out, literally. It is tempting to avoid all the drama and tears and simply sneak out. This is a short-term fix and unadvisable. Leaving without saying good-bye is sneaky and can easily erode the feelings of trust you have worked so hard to establish. In the long run, your child will become more insecure and experience stronger anxiety if you sneak out.

Stand Your Ground

Because separations are often emotional and trying to both you and your child, you may easily find yourself swayed by your child's demands. Requests for "just one more kiss" or "five more minutes" are difficult to refuse. Again, in the long run, this often makes matters worse. You will find that good-byes will become easier if you stay the course and leave promptly after you say you will.

Of course, you want to be reassuring if your child is having a fit when it is time to say good-bye. Be firm and direct in explaining to your child what is happening. It may be helpful if your child has a clear sense of where you will be and what you will be doing while you are apart. You may even wish to show him your place of work or other setting so he can form a mental image of where you'll be. If your child is too young to understand time, use a concrete reference: "I'll be home after you eat lunch," or "When Sesame Street is over, you know it will be time for me to return."

Separation anxiety, as with other normal childhood behaviors, will fade over time. Be sure to recognize your child's progress and reassure her by helping her to remember that you always return when you say you will. As she matures, the assurance that you will remain a stable source of love and comfort, even when you are not there, will allow her to say good-bye with ease and rejoice when she sees you again.

 **Fact**

Establishing a routine adds predictability and a sense of security to separations. Maybe you can designate a special window for waving good-bye, or set a practice of just "two hugs and a kiss." One cute idea is to kiss the child's palm and close his fingers in. Explain to the child that now if he needs a kiss from you, he has one for later.

CHAPTER 7

It's All Mine: Possession Tantrums

"Mine!" This may be a frequent demand that you hear from your toddler. He may adamantly claim ownership, even if something does not belong to him. She may frequently grab toys from other children or insist that items that she sees in the store are for her. Sharing is difficult, if not impossible. When you ask your child to share, a raging temper tantrum may occur. Why is sharing such a difficult task for toddlers? Is there anything you can do to make it easier?

The Egocentric Child

One major reason that your young child has difficulty sharing is that she is egocentric. Egocentrism is not the same as selfishness. Rather, egocentrism refers to the inability to understand another person's perspective. Toddlers see and understand the world through only their own eyes. This self-centered perception fades as the child matures but generally will last until the child is in elementary school.

Your Child Is the Reason

In fact, your egocentric child may attribute himself to be the direct reason or cause of many things that occur in his life. He may believe that the weather is warm because he wants to go swimming, or that the local public television station is airing Barney because it is his favorite show. When your child is egocentric, he

sees himself as the reason or cause for negative events as well. One mother remembers, "One day, when I went to pick up my son from preschool, I found him to be very upset. I saw that there was a substitute teacher and thought that maybe she had upset my son in some way. Once he was home, my son started to tell me that he was very sorry for what he had done to Miss Othamyer (his regular teacher). When I pushed him for details, he told me that the substitute had told him Miss Othamyer was sick that day. He then started to cry again and repeated that it was all his fault. Finally, he revealed why he felt guilty. The day before, he had felt angry with his teacher and had secretly wished for a new teacher. Now he was convinced that his wish had made Miss Othamyer ill!"

I Cannot See It Your Way

Not being able to comprehend what someone else is seeing, hearing, or feeling makes social relationships very difficult. Your child will not be able to interpret her friends' actions or motivations realistically. Her friend announces that he is not feeling well, and that he wants to go home. Your egocentric child may not understand her friend's feelings, and may believe that the friend is leaving because he wishes to make her sad.

 Essential

Quite literally, your young child sees himself as the center of the world. This immature perception may lead him to believe that all the toys in the store are there for him, or that your only role in life is to care for him.

You See It My Way

When your child is egocentric, she will not be able to step outside of her own perception to understand your viewpoint. Consequently, this means that she will assign her own viewpoint to you. Quite literally, this means that she believes that you see what she sees, hears, and feels. If you were to ask your child to show you the page of a picture book, she might hold it up so that the requested page is facing her. She is operating on the assumption that if she can see the page, so can you. She may also "hide" by closing her eyes. After all, if she is not able to see you, then you cannot see her.

The egocentric child, believing that others know what he knows, may communicate in a very egocentric fashion. He does not consider the listener's perspective. For example, when you pick up your child at child care, she may start whining, "Cindy says I am not allowed!" She is assuming you know who Cindy is, what it is that she is forbidding, and that you know why this would be upsetting. Another example is when your child approaches you, visibly distraught, and says, "Help me find it." Again, your child takes it for granted that you will know what "it" is.

You may observe two young children engaging in what appears to be a conversation. When you listen carefully, instead of hearing a dialog, you may hear a "collective monologue." Both children may be taking turns speaking, but there is not true interactive give-and-take. Each child is simply saying what she wishes to say, without listening or accounting for her friend's perspective.

A collective monologue may sound something like this:

Child A: We got a new kitty in my house.
Child B: I like dogs. I want a dog.
Child A: My kitty is so very soft.
Child B: Power Rangers! I want a Power Ranger toy.
Child A: Her name is Patches.
Child B: I call the Power Ranger Jack.

For as long as your child is egocentric, she will assume that everyone else knows how she feels and that everyone feels the same way that she does. This limitation makes it very difficult for

her to share. For her to want to share, she needs to see the perspective and wishes of the other person; she needs to develop empathy.

Empathy

Empathy, the ability to truly understand or relate to what someone
else is feeling, is difficult for a child who is egocentric. However,
there are ways that you can help your child to become empathetic.
The ability to empathize with another person's feelings will help your
child develop a willingness to share. She will not wish to share a toy
with another child unless she can understand how the other child
feels about having an opportunity to play with that toy. Additionally,
when your child is empathetic, she is better equipped to manage
social interactions and conflicts. In order to compromise, a child
must be aware of the other person's wishes or needs. Additionally,
cooperation requires a person to step out of her sole perspective and
see the problem from a group perspective.

 **Fact**

Empathy is different from sympathy. Sympathy—feeling for someone else's feelings—is sometimes an easier concept for young children. With empathy, though, they can actually put themselves in
that person's place and feel what that person is feeling.

Early Empathy

Empathy is a skill that develops slowly over time. Even a child
who is egocentric may show empathy on occasion. Children as young
as twelve months to fifteen months may show some awareness and
sensitivity to the emotions of others around them. When infants were
shown videos of children crying, the infants began to show signs of
distress such as fussiness or crying.

By the time your child is two or three years old, you may begin to witness some prosocial behavior. Some children may even occasionally show signs of true compassion and empathy. You may witness your child responding with empathy when another person is hurt or upset. She may ask that person if he's okay, or may even offer a toy or a hug.

It is important to note that your young child is still trying to understand and manage her feelings. Although you may occasionally see empathetic responses and acts of kindness, your child probably will not consistently exhibit this trait until she is six or seven years of age.

Promoting Empathy

You can help your child learn to recognize others' feelings and perspectives by deliberately pointing out how the other person may be feeling: "Look how Grandma is smiling. I bet she is happy to see you." "I see that the baby is fussy and rubbing his eyes. That usually means that he is tired." You can even make a game by identifying the feelings and perspective of TV or book characters: "How do you think Goldilocks felt when the bears came home?" or "I bet Cookie Monster is excited to go to the bakery."

 **Essential**

You can set the stage for empathy and care early on. Consider involving your toddler in simple tasks or small jobs. By asking her to be a caregiver and to help water plants or feed the pet, you can talk about how your child's behavior has an effect on someone or something else: "See how Rover wags his tail when you brush him? That means that you make him feel happy."

You have a great opportunity to promote empathy when your child has a conflict or hurts someone else. When possible, encourage the victim to tell your child how he feels. "You bit me! That hurt, and now I am angry!" When the victim is unable to speak, you can give the victim words. For example, "You grabbed the doll away from your sister, and now she is crying. That is her way of telling you, 'Stop! You are hurting me!'"

You can further help your child become sensitive to the viewpoint of the other person by involving her in helping the victim. This will also help her see the consequences of her behavior. Ways that your child can help her victim may include bringing a bandage or ice or perhaps simply offering a hug.

Resist the temptation to force your child to apologize. Saying, "I am sorry" has little meaning to a young child unless he truly understands how his behavior hurt the other person and he feels remorseful. Having your child recite an apology may send him the message that it is okay to act as he did as long as he apologizes afterward. You may, however, prompt your child to share his feelings: "How do you feel, now that you see that you have hurt Thomas?" If he is indeed remorseful or sorry, then by all means, he should express that. Apologies are only meaningful when they come from the heart.

Why Your Child Owns Everything

When your child starts to claim objects as "mine," he has achieved an important developmental milestone. He is now developing a strong sense of his own unique identity. He is himself and is separate from you. He must first have the concept of "me" before he has the concept of "mine." He may then equate his possessions as part of his identity and who he is. Early on, he will see his possessions as an extension of himself and may not make a distinction between "my hair, my eyes, my doll." They may all be a part of his identity.

Only when your child understands that she can own something will she be able to understand that she can allow someone to use it and that she then can reclaim it. She then may become very attached to a possession, and sharing may be very difficult. It may be helpful to reassure your child that the object that she shares will be cared for and dutifully returned to her. She needs to know that even when someone else is playing with her toy, she always retains ownership.

Before Conflicts Arise

As with many issues, prevention is often the first step in managing temper tantrums that are caused by sharing. There are specific ways that you can help prevent conflict. Additionally, you can promote the development of early skills that will help your child learn to share.

Prevention

Set a good example. You will have many opportunities to be a good role model for sharing behaviors. Share freely with your child and tell him why: "I am going to let you wear my scarf today. I will be happy that it will help keep you warm." Take the time to point out to your child when he can observe that other people are sharing: "That was nice of Grandma, she shared her cookies with us." "Mr. McGregor is letting us have a turn to use his garden rake, so I can clean up the backyard."

Sharing is difficult for young children. They will not freely and willingly share until they are no longer egocentric and have mastered skills in turn-taking and social interaction. Sometimes, it may be best to avoid requiring your child to share. When you know that your child will be playing with other children, try to have many toy and activity choices available. If possible, have duplicates of items that you know will be in high demand.

 **Essential**

Your child may feel better if she can set aside a few treasured possessions that can be declared off-limits for sharing. Be sure to warn your child when there will be times that she is expected to share, such as when she brings a toy to her child care program for show-and-tell.

Prepare your child in advance. If your child is going to have a play date, take a moment to talk with him. Explain to him that his friend will probably wish to have a turn playing with his toys. Reassure him that his friend will not harm the toy or take it home. He will always maintain ownership of his own toy.

Ready for Turn Taking

You can help your child to feel more comfortable with sharing by introducing her to the concept of turn taking early on. The more opportunities your child has with the give-and-take of turn taking, the more willing she may be to understand that sharing does not mean relinquishing ownership.

There are many fun, hands-on play activities that you can use to engage your child in turn taking. Be sure to verbalize "my turn" and "now it is your turn" as you play these simple games.

- Take turns tossing a beach ball back and forth.
- Take turns rolling a toy car back and forth.
- Use a toy telephone to practice the give-and-take of conversation.
- Play a passing game like Hot Potato.
- Play a simple card game such as War or Go Fish.

Waiting for a turn may still be challenging for a young child who has a short attention span or is impatient. You will find guidelines for helping your child to wait his turn in Chapter 10.

Specific Difficulties with Sharing

Your young child will probably be resistant to sharing and may have sharing temper tantrums until she is five or six years old. It is important to realize that your child's emotional response is likely to be influenced by both her temperament and current mood. Although almost all young children have difficulty sharing, there are many different ways that your child may exhibit her anxiety or reluctance to share.

Walking Away

Your child has a friend over to visit for the afternoon. Your child is happily playing with her Legos at the kitchen table, and her friend is quietly watching her. You ask your child to share some of the Legos with her friend. Your child does not seem to become overly upset. However, instead of sharing, she puts her work back into the bin and leaves the table. This is her way of saying that she is not ready to share. It is okay to accept this response. Simply acknowledge her action by saying something like, "I can see that you chose to find a new activity rather than sharing the Legos. I am glad that you will let your friend have a turn, and I am sure you will rejoin her when you wish."

Wanting It Back

Your child has been pushing a toy car around the base of the tree. He then leaves it and starts to play with a dump truck instead. All is calm until his sister walks over and picks up the car. "Mine!" he screams. "I had that!" He still wants to play with the dump truck, but he wishes to maintain control over and a sense of ownership of the toy car. In the interest of fairness, you may explain to him that, if he wants another turn, then he will have to wait until his sister has had a turn.

If this seems to be a recurring problem for him, you can try to prevent it. When he appears to have stopped playing, you can ask him, "Are you sure that you are finished? If you stop playing with this toy, that means that you are ready to let someone else have a turn." There may still be times when he will change his mind, but this should help reduce the incidents.

Hoarding Toys

Sometimes, when your child is unwilling to release control of toys, she may hoard them. If she is hoarding toys, she is not really playing with them. You may see that she is simply collecting toys and holding on to as many as she can. Some children literally carry handfuls of toy pieces or cram toys into their pockets. Alternatively, she may be putting them in a hiding place or personal place to prevent other children from playing with them. You will need to intervene and help her make choices and then become involved with play. Try saying, "Let's find one toy that you can sit down and play with. You will have a chance to have a turn with one of the other toys after this activity."

Grabbing

Young children often grab toys away from other children. Egocentrism makes it hard for them to realize how their actions hurt the other child. You can bring this to their attention by saying something like, "When you grab the ball away from Lori, she feels sad. Can you see that she is crying? I'll bet you would be sad if someone grabbed a ball away from you."

Alert!

Remember, your child learns from your behavior as much as she does from your words. Avoid grabbing the toy away from her. You send her a mixed message if you grab a toy from her while you are telling her that grabbing is an unacceptable behavior.

Another reason that your young child is grabbing toys away from other children is that your child has a limited ability to communicate his needs or wants. With your guidance, he can learn to use words instead of grabbing. For example, you witness your child approach another child in the sandbox. He quickly reaches over and pulls a shovel away from the other child. You may say, "I can see that you wish to have a turn using that shovel. This child here was having a turn. You may not grab the shovel from her. If you want a turn, you need to use words. Now, let's return the shovel, and then you can ask for a turn." If your child is very young, you may need to suggest words that he can use: "Let's ask this child, 'Can I have a turn?'"

Helping Your Child Share

If your child is in a situation in which she is having a hard time sharing, there are some things that you can do. First, if your child is having a full-blown tantrum over sharing, you will need to help her calm down. Your attempts at reasoning with her will be fruitless if she has lost emotional control. You will not be able to guide her through any conflict resolution when she is overwhelmed with feelings of anger or frustration.

 Essential

> Do not force your young child to share. Encouragement is fine, but coercion will only cause your child to feel anger and resentment. Ultimately, your child will learn to share for intrinsic reasons, such as a wish to make a friend happy.

When your child is having a hard time sharing a toy, you may find improvement if you use the term turn taking instead of sharing. The connotation is slightly different. Consider, if you share your ice cream, you lose part of it. Conversely, if you allow someone to have a turn with your blocks, the implication is that the blocks will be returned. Additionally, sharing may be tolerable if you can reassure your child that the item will be well cared for and that she, too, will have a turn.

When your child is in a battle with another child over a possession, there may be times when you will need to step in. You do not want to automatically solve all of your child's problems for her. Whenever possible, allow her and her friend to work through the conflict. She needs the direct hands-on experience of negotiation and resolving conflicts with her peers. There will be times, of course, that you may need to assist them.

Here are some guidelines for when to intervene during a sharing conflict:

- When either of the children seems emotionally out of control.
- When it is apparent that the conflict could escalate into violence.
- When the same conflict keeps recurring.
- When the children's resolutions continuously result in one of the children's being a victim or a loser.

When you do intervene, resist rushing in and making it all better immediately. Your role is to help the children by guiding them in the conflict-resolution process. Avoid asking the children, "Who had it first?" as this is bound to cause the children to blame or accuse each other, thereby only escalating the conflict. Start by clarifying or restating the problem: "Okay, it seems that both you and Joseph want to have a turn on the bicycle." Then you can prompt the children to explore potential solutions by asking them questions: "Can you think of a way that both of you can ride the bicycle?" "How can you find a fair answer so that you both will be satisfied?" "What can you do while Joseph is taking his turn?" Then guide them to follow through with their own solutions.

CHAPTER 8

I Am a Big Kid Now: Power Struggle Tantrums

Is he really in the terrible twos? Your once happy-go-lucky baby is now defiant and negative. Her moods change like the wind. One minute she desperately wants you to hold her, and the next minute she is squirming out of your grasp and running from you. One minute she insists on pouring her own juice, and the next minute she is screaming for help to use a spoon. When you learn why she is behaving this way, you will be on the way to turning those terrible times into terrific ones.

Why Is My Toddler So Moody?

Toddlerhood is an amazing stage in your child's development. It is quite literally a stage of transition and transformation. Your toddler is in between infancy and full-fledged childhood. In many ways, he is still a dependent infant and he needs your care and support. However, he is on the cusp of childhood. Now he is walking. He's learning self-help skills such as dressing, grooming, and even toilet use. He is beginning to reach out and try his many new skills. He is eager to announce, "I am a big kid now!"

This time of in-between is often a time of confusion, ambivalence, and emotional conflict for your child. One major cause of this is her growing independence from you. Consequently, she is quickly developing her own sense of personal identity. She is exploring issues such as, "Who am I?" "How am I the same as or different from

Mom?" "What are my own preferences and desires?" This exploration can sometimes lead to power struggles. Toddlers are coming to terms with the idea that, although they may be separate from you, they still desperately need you.

Fact

It is believed that a child's awareness of his own separate identity and sense of "self" do not emerge until the second year of life. Studies show that children under the age of twelve to sixteen months did not even recognize themselves in the mirror, believing the reflection to be a different child.

The Desire for Power

You may be surprised to see someone as small and as young as your toddler engage you in a power struggle. However, many toddlers do begin to battle for power and then they throw temper tantrums when their efforts are thwarted.

Power Struggles

Toddler power struggles are a natural progression in your child's development. She is discovering that she can use her mind, words, and body to make things happen. At this time, she is beginning to recognize that she is an individual. She is aware that her tastes and preferences are uniquely hers. Although she is still egocentric, she can understand that others may not share her tastes or wishes. Not everyone likes cold French fries or playing in the mud the way that she does. She naturally has the urge to test her newfound skills and express her ideas and preferences. From her perspective, she knows that adults are bigger, stronger, make the decisions, and have power. So far, you have directed all of her choices and actions. However, along with the urge to be a "big kid" comes the desire to share in some of that power. As you might expect, the process for her to learn the limits of her power may not be smooth. When she naturally discovers she cannot do all that she wants to do, she is bound to feel angry and frustrated.

Learning that you cannot always get what you want is one of life's big lessons. There will surely be times when you must deny your child's wishes, but this does not always have to become an unpleasant confrontation. Conflicts with your toddler can be win-win. Like arguments, power struggles require two sides. You do not have to give in to your child's demands, nor do you have to overpower your child. You can use positive alternatives such as trying to reach a compromise with your toddler, or distract his attention and redirect it. Here are some examples: "Three cookies will spoil your appetite, but I can let you have one to tide you over." "You cannot play with my vase, but here are some of your stacking cubes for you to play with instead."

 Essential

Your child does not want full control and ultimate authority and power. In fact, he still needs the comfort of knowing that someone who loves him will guide him and keep him safe. Being in control and feeling like he has some control can be quite different.

Empowering Your Child

In order for your child to have a sense of power, she needs to

- Feel she can do what she sets out to do
- Believe she can influence people and events
- Have some influence over decisions that affect her

Find ways for your child to feel powerful. Let him be in charge of adults during a very simple task. For example, maybe he can choose what color place mat everyone has at the dinner table. Other small decisions that you could let your child make may include how many tulips to plant in the garden or what card to send Grandma for her birthday. Start involving him in some family decision making. For example, if you are gathered to decide on which movie to rent for the evening, ask for his opinion, too. You do not have to honor his choice, just be sure to let him know that his voice is heard and his preferences are considered.

Increasing Independence

Just a few months earlier, you saw your child hesitantly take her first steps toward independence or autonomy. You have probably witnessed that, in novel or scary situations, she stayed very close to you. Once comfortable, she may have ventured out, often returning to you for reassurance and comfort.

Now your child is bolder. With less hesitation, she may venture farther away from you. She feels safe as long as she knows that you are right there. As time passes, you will see your toddler separate more quickly from you and show more ease at independently exploring her environment and interacting with other people.

This growing independence is not a smooth process. Your child may easily follow the urge to boldly venture farther away, as a big kid would. However, it is possible that she will change her mind abruptly. Feeling suddenly vulnerable, she might realize that maybe she went too far out of her comfort zone. It is as if your child gleefully ran in to the waves at the beach, only to discover she is now in over her head. Predictably she panics and then scrambles to quickly return to the shore and safety. Likewise, the realization of having wandered too far from your side can induce anxiety or panic—two very strong emotions that can be overwhelming for your child.

Your child is trying to find that fine balance between being an independent and self-assured "big kid" and being a baby needing your comfort and reassurance. You may witness this ambivalence and conflict as your child literally seems to try to run from you and toward you at the same time.

The following common scenario is an example of separation ambivalence. Your toddler is refusing to leave the playground with you. With a show of confident bravado, she runs away from you when you go after her. The more you yell and chase, the more she runs. You finally stop and call out, "I am not chasing you anymore; I am going to leave." Suddenly, your once-bold rebel transforms into a dependent baby again. With tears flowing, she pleads, "Wait! Here I come," and she now comes running back to you.

Fighting for Autonomy

Sometime after your child's first birthday, he will start to yearn for autonomy. Your toddler is eager to be a "big kid" and he wants to try out and subsequently master many of the new motor, cognitive, and social skills that children rapidly develop at this stage. Exploring their environment and curiosity or interest in people helps children use the skills they're building.

Alert!

Toddlers are famous for their boundless energy. They are now hopping, running, and climbing all over the place. As a result, children of this age are more likely to find themselves in dangerous situations because they are unable to gauge their own ability and monitor their actions. Without parental supervision, they can easily find themselves in situations requiring them to be rescued.

What the Battle Looks Like

For many toddlers, the desire for autonomy becomes a very strong urge. You will clearly know if your child is making a bid for autonomy through her words and actions. Her favorite phrase is now "me do!" She might refuse your help with simple tasks, often resisting your attempts to feed or dress her. A simple chore like putting on her jacket can now spark a battle. She squirms, kicks, and whines, fighting to do it herself. When you relent and give her the jacket, she has great difficulty. She may have one arm in backward or upside down before she becomes completely frustrated. She then backs down and asks for your help. Battles for independence like these may be a part of your daily life with your toddler. With many toddlers, this urge may result in your child's often wanting to do much more than she is capable of doing. Toddlers are often interested in trying activities that are well beyond their physical or developmental abilities. They do not have a clear sense of their own limitations. You may see your child trying to lift a heavy box. She may want to tackle adult activities such as washing dishes or using the VCR.

Your Child Needs to Win

Achieving autonomy is an important developmental task for your child. He needs to begin experiencing success in his attempts to master new skills independently. When your child is allowed appropriate opportunities to act independently, he will develop a lasting confidence and sense of self-reliance.

 Essential

Toddlers are very rigid in their thinking. If you let them do something once, they may insist on doing it every time. This could be a problem if you let her flush the toilet and then she insists on doing it whenever anyone uses the bathroom. You will need to gently explain that there are times when she needs to let an adult do some things.

How you respond to your child's battle for autonomy will influence his development. You can help him feel successful and competent by allowing him some opportunities to act independently and make some limited choices. If you restrict your child from his autonomy by being overprotective, you may notice, at first, that your child will become more insistent that you allow him some freedom. The battles will increase in frequency and intensity. Eventually, your child will give up. He may develop a lowered self-esteem and could doubt his ability to be independent. In fact, he may even become more dependent on you than ever before. He may regress in behavior and revert to wanting his bottle again, or he may lose ground in toilet training.

Problems may also arise if your child has some opportunities to act independently but you punish him or harshly criticize him for mistakes or accidents (spilling, wetting, and breaking things). Then your toddler may come to doubt his competence or he might be fearful to show any initiative. Toddlers who are restricted from developing autonomy early on in their development often become preschoolers who are hesitant to try new things or school-agers who always ask for help with even the simplest tasks. For example, if your seven-year-old still asks you to brush his teeth for him, he has probably become too reliant on adult help and has not developed autonomy.

Allowing for Independence

In order to help your child develop autonomy with minimal tantrums, you need to learn to let go and let your child start to do some things on her own. Encouraging her attempts while promoting her sense of initiative will build her confidence.

Set the Stage
You can easily set the stage for your child to be independent. Focus on daily living or self-help skills first. For example, you can help your child be more independent while getting dressed. Here are

some specific ways that you can prepare everything so she can manage most of the task without your help.

- Have her outfit laid out in advance.
- Select clothing that does not have many zippers, buckles, or buttons. Overalls can be a nightmare—stick with simple items. Pants with elastic bands and pullover tops are good to start with.
- Wherever you can, replace smaller fasteners such as buttons or snaps with Velcro. If you sew, you can make buttonholes larger and sew on larger, more manageable buttons.
- Attach a key ring to the end of a zipper so that it is easier to grasp.
- Attach buttons or large beads to the end of drawstrings so that they are not pulled through.
- For clothing that looks the same on both sides, sew or use indelible ink to mark an X on the back seam.
- Teach your child the easy way to put on his coat: Lay the unfastened coat on the floor. The child stands at the top of the coat (near the hood), leans over and places his arms in the armholes, and then flips the coat over his head.

You can also set the stage for your child's attempts at independence in the following activities: toilet use, mealtimes, and daily hygiene and grooming routines. Start simple and add complexity as your child's skills and confidence grow.

Challenges

Sometimes it may be challenging for you to stand back as your child attempts new tasks and skills on her own. Your child will make mistakes along the way. For example, she may put her shoes on the wrong feet or put too much toilet paper in the toilet. Additionally, be prepared for most of your child's attempts to be messy endeavors. While your child is learning to use silverware or brush her teeth, there are bound to be some mishaps. Learn to take them in stride.

Nobody learns by doing something perfectly the first time around.

Whenever possible, avoid becoming impatient with your child's attempts. When you become impatient and take over the task, your child may doubt her ability. She may start to see her own attempts at autonomy as displeasing to you, and she may be hesitant to try new tasks in the future.

When You Must Intervene

There will surely be times when it may not be practical to allow your child to do something without your help. If your child could be injured or you cannot wait for him, you may have to intervene. For example, you could say, "I know that you want to put your shoes on by yourself, but we are running late. If I do not help you, you will miss the bus. Next time, we will start earlier so you can have time to put your shoes on by yourself." Be sensitive to the fact that this may be particularly frustrating for her. You may be able to diffuse a tantrum by offering a compromise. For example, "I know that you can do a good job putting your shoes on. Today we will need to be fast. Perhaps we can work together to be fast? I will hold each shoe open while you push your foot in."

Negativity

By showing negativity or opposition to you, your child asserts his own awakening sense of power and control. The mantra for this stage is the word no. It may even seem that this has become your child's favorite word. It is often, literally, their declaration of independence. He has discovered that, when he uses the word no, he has the power to negate your guidance while expressing his own wishes or preferences. You may even discover that your child will say no to a suggestion that you know he actually wants to accept. You may offer a dream come true: "Would you like to go to Disneyland and eat pizza every day?" and he will still say no. To the extreme, some children will shift their wishes just to be in opposition to yours. For example, you say, "Okay, it is time to go inside." Your child says, "No!" "All right then, you can stay outside," you reply. However, your child answers, "No, I don't want to." When this happens, do not allow yourself to be drawn into an argument. If you can, give him a choice; if not, simply make a choice for him.

 **Fact**

You may feel strongly about your child telling you no. It is important to remember that, at this age, she is not being spiteful. She may be being disagreeable, but she is not being disrespectful.

Your child may also choose to assert her power and control through nonverbal means. Nonverbal negativity behavior could include:

- Running from you when you tell him it is time to leave the playground.
- Going limp when you try to get her to walk into the doctor's office.
- Tensing his leg muscles and becoming rigid when you try to get him into the car seat.

There are some ways you can reduce your child's negativity. Be a good role model. Most parents do find they spend a lot of time restricting their toddler's behavior by using directives such as "no," "stop," or "don't." Try to reduce the number of times you have to say no to your child. You can do this by structuring his environment and removing hazards. When you do this, you provide freedom and safety for your child to explore. This will also foster her sense of autonomy. Try to state your expectations clearly: "Don't sit on the couch" can become "I need you to sit in your chair." Whenever possible, offer your child a choice. "Stop throwing sand" can become "You can use the sand to build either castles or roads, but you must keep the sand in the box."

The Power of Choice

Giving your child choices is a powerful way for you to eliminate much of your child's negativity and oppositional behavior. When your child has some choices, she has a sense of autonomy and power. Additionally, when your child makes a choice, then she has ownership of the choice she made and will be more likely to comply.

Consider carefully how much choice you are going to give your child. Choice is power. While giving your child some choices can be a valuable way to reduce power struggles in toddlers, you are not handing them the reins. Ultimately, you are still in control. There are many things that are not negotiable. When it comes to issues regarding your child's health and safety, for example, what you say goes. For example, you may allow your child to choose what color sweater she wants to wear or what brand of cereal she eats for breakfast. However, you do not let her choose whether to wear a sweater when it is cold or whether to eat a nutritious breakfast. Be sure to explain to your child, "I cannot offer you a choice about this. This is important for your health."

Real Choices

Do not give your child a choice unless there really is one present. You may inadvertently find yourself doing this by phrasing a request so that it sounds like a choice: "Wouldn't you like to come inside now?" or "Do you want to clean up your room, please?" Are you prepared for him to say no? When you give your child a choice, you must be prepared to honor his choice. This is also true even if your child chooses the option you did not anticipate. For example, "Either you can sit still at the circus or we are going home." If your child chooses to go home, then you need to follow through.

Limited Choices

Too many choices can be overwhelming for your child. Broad choices such as, "What do you want to eat for breakfast?" or "Where do you think we should go for the weekend?" do not help guide your child's behavior and may be hard for you to honor. What if your child asks for chocolate icing for breakfast or to go to Disneyworld for the weekend?

The key is to offer your child a limited choice. A limited choice gives your child two positive alternatives. Both alternatives are ones that you are prepared to accept. You have a predetermined expectation of how you want your child to behave, and you allow her to make choices within those parameters. For example, you want your child to eat a nutritious breakfast. You say, "Which do you want for breakfast—waffles or pancakes?" Of course, your toddler may still ask for chocolate icing. If this happens, remind her, "That is not one of your choices; you may choose either waffles or pancakes." There are many limited choices you can give your child each day. White socks or blue socks? Wheat bread or rye bread? Ponytail or braids?

 *Question?*

What is a false choice?
A false choice is when only one of the alternatives is positive or feasible to your child: "You can clean your room or I will ground you" or "You can get out of the pool or I will pull you out." These "choices" are set up to ensure your child will comply with your wishes, but they do not give your child any sense of freedom or power.

When you give your child a limited choice, you help him:

- Comply with the behavior you want
- Feel independent and empowered

- Mitigate his urge for power struggles
- Understand expectations

The Illusion of Choice

There may be times when your young child is being oppositional over a behavior where there is no choice. Some parents find they can use a technique called the illusion of choice. Here, both choices you offer result in the same behavior that you want. However, the child is still permitted to feel some sense of power. For example, you want your child to take her allergy pill and she has clenched her jaw shut. The "choice" you give her may be, "You can take your pill with water or juice." The focus changes. The issue now is not whether she will take the pill, but the inconsequential choice of beverage.

Following Through

Along with the freedom of having a choice comes the responsibility to be accountable for the decision made. Not only should you honor your child's choice, but you need to be sure he does as well. You may find that your child sometimes has difficulty deciding and he wavers, and you will have to set a limit. One mother shares, "Every choice I gave my daughter became a huge deal. I would ask if she wanted saltines or graham crackers for snack. Her typical response would be, 'Umm, saltines! No, graham crackers. No wait, saltines. Saltines, really saltines.' I would have the box out of the cabinet and she would throw a fit, crying for graham crackers." If your child has a hard time sticking with her choice, you may need to help her follow through. Advise your child to consider her choice carefully. Let her know that what she chooses is what she will get. Once she makes the choice, restate her choice as a conclusion: "Okay, you chose saltines. That is what you are going to have." If she balks at this, say, "This time you have chosen saltines. You may choose graham crackers next time."

CHAPTER 9

At a Loss for Words: Emotional Tantrums

Y ou are at the playground with your two-year-old son. He seems to be happily engaged building roads in the sandbox. You are watching him carefully from a nearby bench when he suddenly begins to cry and wail. You run over, perplexed by his behavior—there seems to be no reason for this outburst. Did a bee sting him? Is he frustrated because the sand will not stay as he wants it to? What is wrong? If only he could just tell you!

Frustration with Language Skills

It can be very frustrating and scary when you cannot communicate to get your needs met. This is particularly true for very young children who are not speaking yet. It is unlikely that you can remember what it was like when you did not have language skills to express yourself. Here is a fictional scenario to help you envision and empathize what it could be like for your young child: Imagine that you are fourteen months old and you are sitting in your high chair. Lunchtime has just begun and you are about to grab at the Cheerios on the tray in front of you, when you suddenly feel a sharp pain under your one leg. You do not know what it is (you are probably sitting on a toy), but boy, does it hurt! You start to squirm and move your leg and your mom notices you. "Oh, is my sweetie hungry?" she coos. "Why aren't you eating your cereal?" Since you have no way of answering her, you squirm some more. She continues to talk to you:

"How about some applesauce?" She brings a spoonful of applesauce over. The pain in your leg has ruined any interest in food that you may have had, so you push her hand away. "How about some juice?" she tries. Oh, if only you could tell her! But the only thing you can do is cry. "Sweetie, it's okay, here comes some juice," Mom says as you now begin to frantically kick your legs. If you could, you would scream, "I don't want juice! This chair, is hurting my leg!" She places the sippy cup on your tray. In anger, pain, and frustration, you fling the juice cup to the ground and scream while your mom looks down at you, wondering why you are having a meltdown for no reason.

The Importance of Language

The learning of language is an essential developmental mile-stone. The mastery of language use helps your child represent thoughts and actions with words. Comprehension of language helps children reflect on, and so understand and learn from, past experiences and is essential for communicating their needs, expressing their feelings, and sharing their ideas. Without language, a child has very little capacity for memory. He cannot share what he is thinking or even ask for help.

Essential

Within the first six months, your child will have first experiences with fear, surprise, sadness, contentment, anger, and joy. More complex emotions such as jealousy, shame, empathy, and pride do not emerge until the second or third year of life.

Being Overwhelmed

Contrary to the TV image of a permanently smiling, sunny childhood, children experience a great range of emotions, sometimes with surprising intensity. It is normal for your child to experience many strong emotions, including frustration and anger. Before she can use language to express herself, she will have a difficult time managing and coping with these emotions. The only path she has to vent and express emotional upheavals is a physical outburst complete with tears.

It is easy for your child to become overwhelmed with strong feelings. On top of the triggering emotion, she is feeling out of control and possibly scared. You may even witness her tantrum escalate as she becomes frightened by her own loss of control—so much so that the original trigger for the temper tantrum is forgotten.

Basics of Language Development

Most scientists believe that we have an inborn capacity for language acquisition. However, that is only the beginning. Learning to use language and communicate does not occur on its own. Exposure to and experience with language is necessary. Simply allowing your child to hear language (via adult conversation, radio, TV) is not enough. Language acquisition is an interactive, dynamic process. Your child needs to learn the reciprocity, or turn taking, part of communication as well.

 **Fact**

There are two types of language skills: expressive and receptive. Receptive skills develop more rapidly and include listening comprehension and, later in life, reading. Expressive skills include speaking and, later in life, writing. Your young toddler may be able only to say "ball" but shows understanding when you tell him, "Bring the ball over to me."

Steps in Language Development

Your child's attempt to communicate starts right at that first cry or wail after he's born. Within the next few weeks, you will notice his cries will have special meaning, and they will become easier to decode. Soon, those cries will become coos and then the coos will become words. The journey of language acquisition has begun.

Before your child is using words, you will find it helpful to pay particular attention to his body language. A child who is calm and happy will appear relaxed, and his arms and legs will usually be loose and to his sides. If your child is alarmed or scared, she may tense up and pull her arms and legs in. If your child is in pain, she may curl up or rub and pull the affected body part.

The rate in which children acquire language skills varies greatly. Your child may or may not fit into the averages shown in the table.

Language Milestones	
Age	**Ability**
Birth	Responds to human voice
6 weeks–4 months	Coos using vowel sounds (ahh, ee)
5–8 months	Begins using consonant sounds (b, d, g, k, m, p)
7–10 months	Shows understanding of basic words
9–14 months	Says first meaningful word
12–16 months	Follows simple commands (sit down, come here)
16–19 months	Has vocabulary of 5–25 words; starts to use verbs
18–26 months	Combines two words and creates sentences
20–24 months	Labels basic objects
22–26 months	Vocabulary 150–400 words; 60 percent of speech is understandable
33–38 months	Understands basic prepositions (in, under)
36–40 months	Vocabulary 800–1,200 words; 90 percent of speech is understandable

Essential

You can decode your baby's cries. Of course, each child is different, but there are some common cries you may observe. A sharp, high-pitched cry often means that your baby is in pain or distress. Hunger cries are often rhythmic and have a wailing tone. Long, drawn-out cries that have a whiney tone may indicate that your baby is overtired.

Ooh, Ahhh What?

Anywhere from six weeks to four months of age, you will observe your child cooing with vowel sounds. She will be more inclined to do this when she is happy. At around five to seven months of age, consonant sounds will appear, and soon your child will be babbling.

Babbling is more than just stringing random sounds together. You will eventually notice that although not understandable, it sounds as if your child is talking. When children babble, they use the intonation, tone, and cadence of the language they hear around them. The babbling infant raised in a Japanese-speaking home sounds distinctly different from an infant raised in a French-speaking home. In the midst of this stream of babbling, you may hear recognizable words. Maybe your child will say something like this, "Ahh-penee-denee-danee-dada-pada!" Daddy will be excited; however, this is not your child's first word.

The First Word

Officially, your child's first word is when she says it in a meaningful context; for instance, when your child states the name of something while holding on to it or pointing to it. Your child's first word is likely to be a noun, either the name of a beloved caregiver or a label for something present and important in her everyday life. Many first words follow the simple consonant-vowel, consonant-vowel configuration (mama, baba).

 **Question?**

Why is mama not the most popular first English word?
Mama is a very popular first word but often loses the race to Dada. This seems to be because the mother is usually the primary caregiver and usually does not speak in the third person. Instead of saying to the baby, "Where am I? I am Mama," she is more likely to say, "Where is Dada? Let's go find Dada. There is Dada!"

I Have Something to Say

With your happy responses and reinforcement, your child's vocabulary will blossom. By the age of eighteen months, the average child will be using five to twenty-five words. During this time, your child is using holographic speech. This is when he says only one word, but that single word conveys many different meanings. For example, "bye-bye" could mean "I want to leave," "Don't leave me," "Leave me alone," or simply "Good-bye." Somewhere around sixteen to twenty-four months of age, your child will begin learning vocabulary at an accelerated rate. He may be acquiring as many as nine new words a day. One mother shares how dramatic this can be.

> One evening I told my husband that I was taking our nineteen-month-old daughter with me to do some shopping. I had a change of heart and ended up taking her to a carnival instead. She was very excited when we were there. I took her to the duck pond game and asked her if she wanted to pick a duck. "Duck!" she proudly said. We saw a clown with balloons, and for the first time, she said the words clown and balloons. It was like this all evening. I was not sure whether she was just echoing the words she heard for just one time or if she was really learning them. I soon knew the answer. When we got home, I did not want to admit to my husband that we had gone to the carnival, but my daughter kept calling out her new favorite word: "BINGO," she shouted, "BINGO!"

By the time your child is six years old, he will know approximately 14,000 words! In this same period your child will start linking two and three words together to form sentences. These basic sentences are noun-verb combinations such as "Mama go" or "go doggy." More complex sentences and grammatical usage will develop through the preschool years. As your child's language skills develop, so will her ability to express needs and feelings in an appropriate way rather than having a temper tantrum.

Promoting Language Development

Before you can begin helping your child to use words to manage and communicate strong emotions, you will need to help promote her verbal skills and build her vocabulary. There are many things that you can do to accomplish this. Your child is learning about language and communication long before she says her first words. Remember that receptive language skills develop more rapidly. Your child can understand much more than she can say.

Talk to Baby

Talk to your baby right from the start. The more he is exposed to language, the better. A significant part of his early learning takes place during the warm, loving interactions you share. Interactive games are a great place for you to start. Do not forget the classics such as rock-a-bye baby, peekaboo, or pat-a-cake.

You may be worried that you do not know what to say to your infant. Do not be self-conscious. Your child benefits from even the simplest dialog. Try talking aloud. Think of yourself as a narrator as you describe what is happening with you and your baby. For example, here is what you could say as you are getting her ready for snack: "Are you hungry? I am going to pick you up now and put you in the high chair. I am putting you in the high chair. Look, I am placing the tray on so there will be a place for your food. Here are Cheerios. Ooh, I see that smile! I think you are happy for Cheerios."

You must provide response and reinforcement to promote your child's language development. If your child's first trials at cooing or babbling elicit no response from you, she will soon recognize that she is being ignored and her attempts to communicate will diminish. Instead, answer her. Echo her verbalizations or add to the dialog. You can playfully say something like, "Did you say oommee? I heard you say oommee! Let me hear you say oommee!" Even very young infants enjoy verbal games and mimicry. You can also engage your child simply by using verbal noises rather than phonic sounds. Raspberries and lip smacking are fun and easy to imitate.

When your child begins speaking, you can help promote future communication skills. Listen carefully and respond appropriately. Help your child learn the reciprocity of conversation by listening and by asking questions. Avoid yes-or-no questions. Spark an interesting conversation with your child by asking open-ended questions. Good discussion questions could start with "why do you think" or "what would happen if."

Sing to Baby

Music is a wonderful way to expose your child to language. There is a huge selection of children's music available, from nursery rhymes to lullabies. Do not discount "adult" music. There is no rule that says babies should not listen to show tunes or that they will not enjoy jazz.

Do not be afraid to sing to your child. Your child is not a music critic. Share one of your own childhood favorites or ad-lib on your own. Try singing some of your daily dialog with her. The tune "Here

We Go 'Round the Mulberry Bush" is easily adaptable and works well for this: "This is the way we put on our socks, put on our socks, put on our socks . . . [brush our teeth, lay down for a nap] so early in the morning."

Read to Baby

Read to your child. You will help him learn language structure and build vocabulary. Even a young infant benefits from hearing your voice and the soothing rhythm or repetition that occurs in many picture books. Soon you will notice your child focusing more and more on the story itself. Reading to your child has other advantages as well. Story time is a marvelous quality time for bonding and sharing with your child. Additionally, studies show that reading to your child will have a positive impact on his literacy skills later in school.

Help Your Child Use Words

Words give your child power over feelings of anger and frustration. The ability to label his own emotions will help him to develop self-control. Once he can identify his feelings, he can begin to make conscious choices about how to express them.

Labeling Emotions

You can help your child learn to identify and label emotions early on. Start by labeling her emotions for her as you observe them. For example, try saying something like, "Oh, that big smile tells me that you are feeling very happy!" or "I saw you throw that toy. I bet you're angry!" When she begins talking, you can help to restate her words to identify emotions. For example, when your child whines, "I don't want to go to see the doctor," you can respond, "I see you are feeling afraid and worried." This technique is called reflective listening, and you can learn more about it in Chapter 4.

Here is a fun game you can try. Sit down with your child and go through family photo albums or magazine pictures. Have your child guess what the person was thinking or feeling in the picture.

Essential

Help your child label feelings and build vocabulary. Emotional experiences come in a range of intensity; be sure to share these words with your child. When she is mad, is she enraged, furious, angry, or just irritated? When she's happy, is she pleased, glad, thrilled, or ecstatic?

Saying What's on Her Mind

Even if she has the vocabulary, it is likely that your young child will need lots of guidance in order to use these words to express feelings. If your toddler is just starting to speak, you may need to tell her what words to use. If you see her pinch a playmate when the child grabs a toy from her, you can say, "I know you are angry at Max for grabbing the toy. Instead of pinching him, you need to tell him with words. Let's tell Max, 'I'm mad!'" Whenever you coach your child to use specific words, keep the suggested script simple, accurate, and easy to repeat.

This is not something your child will master overnight. There may be many occasions where you need to "give" her words to use. As your child's vocabulary and self-control grow, you will no longer need to give the words, but you still may need to prompt her. You can do this by saying, "You need to tell me why you are crying," "What can you say to Grandma if she is upsetting you?" or, simply, "Use words."

Ways to Express Feelings

Some children, who may be otherwise reluctant to express their feelings, may do so in an indirect fashion. Reluctant or shy children may feel more comfortable expressing themselves by using puppets. Once they put the puppet on their hand, it can do the speaking for them. One mother gives an example of how a toy puzzle was instrumental for her daughter. "We have a 'puzzle' of wooden bears with six interchangeable faces showing different expressions. When my daughter, then not quite three, was playing with it, she put a sad face on the bear. I asked why the bear was feeling sad. She said, 'She is sad because her mummy is shouting.' It certainly was a wake-up call for me, and it enabled her to express feelings in a way that I do not think she would have otherwise."

Understanding Aggression

There are many possible causes for your child to behave aggressively. More often than not, he is lashing out. He is expressing his strong emotions the only way that he is able. Frustration and anger are expressed through hitting, biting, and other aggressive acts when the child is not able to say, "Stop that, you are making me angry!"

 **Fact**

> Your preverbal child is probably not having a tantrum for attention or spite. Your role here is to calmly reassure her and help her regain control. Realize that it may take a while for her to settle down fully. Your patience will pay off.

Here are some examples where lack of language may result in aggressive behavior, and possible ways to respond:

- She grabs a toy away from her younger sister. Say, "I can understand that you want a turn with the toy, but I need you to ask your sister for a turn."
- He shoves another child away while trying to get a seat at the table. Say, "It looks like you are trying to beat your friend to a seat. It is not safe to push. I will show you where you can sit."
- She kicks another child when that child knocked over her block tower. Say, "Boy are you upset! It is okay to be angry when someone wrecks your building, but I will not let you kick him."

- He throws a toy that does not seem to work. Say, "Are you mad that the toy won't go? Perhaps you can ask someone to help when things don't work."

Notice that each example response states the child's emotion or viewpoint. It is important that you recognize and accept your children's feelings. Everyone has the right to feel what he or she feels. You can show acceptance of your child's feelings without accepting his aggressive behavior. In other words, separate the deed from the doer. The underlying message is "I like you, but I don't like it when you _____." You can also see that each response clearly guides the child to a safer and more appropriate response to the child's problem. Your child's emotions have run out of control and turned into a full-scale tantrum; you need to help her put the brakes on her emotions before you can deal with any other issues.

Crying, screaming, and aggression are hard to stop midstream, but here are different strategies you can try to help your child calm down:

- Remain calm. Respond with a calm and quiet voice. If you are emotional or raise your voice, you are likely to fuel the fire.
- Show empathy. Communicate that you are right there and listening: "I know you are feeling _____. I am here to help you."
- Change the venue. Remove your child from a situation or person that is upsetting him. Also, there may be times when you can distract him with humor or a toy.
- Use the power of touch. Try stroking her hair or rubbing his back. Some parents find that they need to hold their child close to help her feel calm and secure.

The Truth about Biting

One of the most troublesome behaviors, from a parent's perspective, is biting. Yet biting is a very common behavior from the time children start teething, through their toddler years.

Why Your Child Bites

In order to control a behavior, you first need to understand why it occurs. Many young children bite when they are overwhelmed with feelings of anger or frustration. This is most likely to be true if your child is impulsive and has yet to learn how to express herself verbally. Biting is a very powerful way to release strong feelings.

Your child may begin teething at four to seven months of age. When her gums are swollen, she may discover that biting can relieve feelings of discomfort and pain.

Children younger than age two or three rely on direct hands-on sensory experiences to form concepts and understanding. This means that they are learning about something if they can see, hear, touch, and so forth. When your child bites you, he may simply be trying to discover, "What will it feel like to bite Mom? How will she taste? How will she react?" Biting usually diminishes once the child acquires verbal skills.

How to Respond to Biting

If you observe your child carefully, you may be able to determine when he is most likely to bite. Perhaps it is when he is tired or over-stimulated. You can then be proactive. Provide your child with that much-needed nap or remove him from the circumstances. You will also know when it is wise to keep an extra eye on him and be available to intervene.

If you suspect teething is the problem, be sure to provide your child with a cool teether or rubber ring. Some parents will attach one to their child's clothing so it is always handy. When your child begins to bite someone, stop him and explain, "Biting hurts people. If you need to bite, use your teething ring. Teething rings are for biting."

Help your child learn consequences and see how their behavior affects someone else. Again, as you stop him from biting, say, "Biting hurts people." You can show him that the victim is crying or that there is a mark on the victim's skin. If the victim is able, ask him to tell the biter that he is hurt. Focus attention on caring for the child who has been bitten. Ask your child to participate in helping the victim feel better. Maybe he can get a Band-Aid or ice or simply offer a hug to the hurt child. Biting, along with other aggressive behaviors, will likely decrease once your child has acquired the adequate language skills he needs to express his emotions and solve his own problems with words.

Alert!

You may have been told to bite your child when your child bites someone. Resist this reaction—it will backfire. Rather than teaching your child that biting hurts, you are sending the message that it is okay to bite someone if she bites you first or if you are angry.

CHAPTER 10

I Can't Wait:
Patience Tantrums

W aiting is difficult for adults as well as for children. The difference is, as an adult, you know that there is a light at the end of the tunnel. When someone says that he will be visiting you next Tuesday, you have a clear sense of how much time that is and you can manage your feelings of anticipation. Not so for your young child who wants what he wants, right now!

How Children Understand Time

For young children, time concepts are very difficult to understand. The passage and measurement of time are abstract concepts. You cannot see, touch, or hear time. Young children fully know and understand only what they have had direct, concrete, hands-on experience with. They have a good concept and understanding of things in their day-to-day world, such as their toys or pet dog. Places, things, or ideas that are outside their direct experience are beyond their true understanding. Time is not only abstract, but changeable: A person's perception of time changes depending on the situation. We all know how time flies when we are having fun, and conversely, how it may seem to pass more slowly when we are waiting. Your child will not be able to fully understand time concepts until he is seven or eight years old.

What Toddlers Know

A toddler's perception of reality is pretty much grounded in the here and now. She is living completely in the moment. Toddlers spend very little time, if any at all, ruminating about the past or worrying and planning for the future. It is unlikely that your toddler is wondering, "Will I be popular in high school?" or "Should I not have bitten Reba last Saturday when she broke my toy?" Concepts such as "a few minutes," "next week," or "later this afternoon" mean very little to toddlers. When they ask you to go to the park and you reply, "Not now, I will take you in a half hour," all they really hear is, "No."

What Preschoolers Know

Your preschooler is starting to understand some basics of the passage of time. She is starting to observe the difference between short and longer periods of time. She will often overgeneralize, referring to all events in the past as if they occurred yesterday, and all events in the future as if they will happen tomorrow. She might still confuse the past and the future. She may say something like, "I am going to Grandma's to visit yesterday." Preschoolers understand concrete time references related to something familiar better than traditional references. For example, "You can have a cookie when Daddy comes home" is more meaningful than "You can have a cookie at four o'clock." "We are going to the circus after you eat lunch" is more meaningful than "We are going to the circus this afternoon." In order to understand your child's concept of time, listen to the words and phrases she uses to describe time: for example, "the other day," "the next day," "before this day," "after this day."

Helping Your Child Delay Gratification

Being patient often means delaying gratification. The ability to delay gratification is closely related to your child's ability to maintain self-control. For your child to delay gratification, she must be able to forego an immediate reward or satisfaction, for a greater payoff later. This ability requires that your child be able to think beyond the here and now and tolerate some frustration. Because an intangible promise of a reward in the future is such an abstract concept, this is a very difficult achievement for young children. To a young child, a bird in the hand is always better than two in the bush.

 **Fact**

Some children have an easier time than others delaying gratification. Temperament plays a role. If your child is generally more impulsive, she will have a more difficult time delaying gratification. Impulsive preschoolers tend to act without thinking, and they expect results without waiting. Additionally, research has shown that children who have formed a secure attachment with their caregivers tend to do better with delaying gratification. They know that eventually, their needs will be met.

The ability to delay gratification is the key to your child's being able to handle impatience and frustration. Recent studies include this ability as part of what psychologists call emotional intelligence. They found that the young child who is able to delay gratification is more likely to be better adjusted, more confident, and more popular as he gets older.

The greatest teacher of this skill is life experience. Each day includes challenges to your child's ability to delay gratification. For example, your child may want a cookie before dinner or to watch TV before finishing his homework. Your essential role here is to avoid giving in to your child's demands. You cannot always protect your children from experiencing frustration and disappointment. Rather than eliminate these experiences, you can help your child understand how time passes, and encourage his patience.

Learning about Time

Helping your child tolerate frustration and impatience will take patience from you. You will not be able to transform your child into a patient child overnight. It is a process that you can help your child with as she matures. You will find that, the more she understands the concepts of time measurement and passage, the more you will see a reduction in impatience tantrums. This process cannot be forced, as a child's understanding of abstract concepts is limited by her cognitive development. Your strategies must be appropriate to her age and developmental progress.

Time Measurement

You can help your child become aware of small units of time with some hands-on activities. This can take place before a child learns to tell time from a clock. Give your child practice with estimating and measuring time. Ask your child to estimate/guess how long an activity or event will take. Time the event or activity to see if he was close. Be sure to discuss the results: "Did it take a longer or shorter time than you guessed? Why do you think that was?"

Here are some simple events or activities that your child may enjoy guessing and timing.

- How long will it take to drive to the park?
- How many minutes does it take for you to brush your teeth?
- How long will the cookies take to bake?
- How many seconds do you think it will take to zip up your coat?
- How many minutes will it be before a commercial comes on TV?

Your child may enjoy playing countdown games with a stopwatch or timer. Ask your child, "How many times can you hop in ten seconds?" "How many blocks can you pick up in one minute?" "How far can you run in twenty seconds?"

Essential

Time is measured in many ways: hours, days, decades, and so forth. When you teach your child about time measurement, it is best to focus on concrete terms that he can relate to. Most of your child's experiences occur within time frames of minutes, hours, or days.

You can also introduce basic time-telling skills to your pre-schooler. Use a large numerical clock face. A toy one that is able to be manipulated works great. Keep it simple at first, using just the hour time for references: "Dinnertime will be when the short arm is pointing to the seven." One clever mother made homemade clock faces out of paper plates and attached cardboard hands with a metal paper fastener. She put these clocks up around the house. She put one over her child's bed and set it to read 8:00, the child's bedtime. She put another by the fish bowl and set it to the time that her son was to feed the fish.

There are ways to help your child understand longer times in a more concrete fashion as well. Try to use references that are relevant to your child's life and experiences. Rather than telling your child that Grandma is coming for a visit in three days, try telling him that Grandma will arrive after he has had three breakfasts. You can mention events further in the future this way as well: "Christmastime will come once the weather turns colder and we put up the decoration lights."

Making a simple calendar with your child is a great way to help her measure time and prepare for future events. For a young child, a one-week calendar is plenty. Let your child decorate the days to signify routine or special events. For example, glue a birthday candle to Tuesday because it is Daddy's birthday. Alternatively, if Saturday is the day you go fishing, your child can color a little fish on that block. As each day passes, ask your child to cross it off the calendar. This is a concrete way for her to measure how many more days until the anticipated event happens.

Alert!

Because of your young child's cognitive limitations, the use of pictures and symbols to measure time will be meaningful only for children older than three or four. Additionally, the use of numbers and letters is more appropriate for children older than six years of age.

Time Passages

Although your child does not see it, the progression of time has a predictable rhythm—the sun rises every morning; summer follows spring. When your child is able to see these rhythms and patterns, or time passages, she will be better able to predict and wait for upcoming events.

The presence of predictable rhythms can be seen in daily life, if you establish and adhere to a daily schedule. Routines and rituals will help your child feel more secure. Soon, she will be able to be patient for an anticipated event when she sees that it falls into a predictable pattern. For example, when Daddy comes home, that means dinnertime will be soon. Daily routines will also help your child understand the concepts of time through sequencing. Your child can easily learn the order of events and whether one event is contingent on another. Your child knows the bedtime routine. First, she has her bath; then she gets into her pajamas. She must brush her teeth before a bedtime story, and finally, Mom tucks her in and turns off the light. You can play an important part in establishing these sequences by sticking to them yourself—a small change in order might seem insignificant to you, but it is important to your child. Using a simple chart with pictures listing these routines can help your child to grasp the idea, and it gives her the opportunity to follow the steps independently.

You can help your child develop patience and reinforce the concept of time passages by introducing him to projects that require a longer period to complete. Gardening is a great example, with the germination, growth, flowering, and fruiting of plants offering daily proof of the passage of time. Your child also has the opportunity to witness the changes in his garden as seasons pass. Other long-term projects that require patience could include putting together a large jigsaw puzzle, baking bread (waiting for the dough to rise before baking), and making clay or papier-mâché crafts (waiting for the project to dry before finishing).

Fact

> You can help reinforce the concept of past and future with your child. Take time at the end of the day to review daily occurrences. Ask your child to reflect on the past—"What did you do today?"—and help him anticipate the near future—"What will you do tomorrow?"

Waiting Games

Waiting is usually an unpleasant and sometimes difficult task for both children and adults. Adults have developed self-control and more patience. They often have mature ways of making waiting more bearable, such as reading, humming a tune to themselves, or daydreaming. Young children have not yet learned ways to manage waiting. Waiting is particularly difficult when your child has only a limited understanding of how long she will have to wait.

Make Waiting Fun

Waiting is part of everyday life. Waiting for lunch to be served, waiting for a turn with a toy, and waiting for a bus are just a few examples that may be part of your child's day. You can cut down on impatience and tantrums by making waiting fun.

Here are some ways to make waiting fun.

- Sing songs.

- Read or tell a story.
- Play a guessing game such as "I Spy."
- Name things that start with the letter ____.
- Play a memory-chain game such as "I am going on a picnic, and I'm going to pack a ____."

A mother of a four-year-old remembers:

> We used to run all of our household errands together one day a week. When it came to short stops such as the post office or the bank, it was often easier for my husband to run in while I sat in the car with my young daughter. She quickly became impatient and whiny until I came up with a waiting game. While on the lookout for Dad to return, we would take turns pointing out strangers on the street. I would point out an elderly woman and exclaim, "Here comes Daddy!" My daughter would giggle madly and she would spot someone else and tell me, "No, here comes Daddy!" The more the person's appearance differed from my husband's, the better.

Are We There Yet?

Traveling may be a true test of your child's patience. Along with waiting, there are other elements that may make traveling difficult for your child. Your child may be very excited to reach the destination, and he may have to remain confined to his seat for a long period of time. In addition, distance is also an abstract concept that is hard for your child to understand. Telling a young child that you have only four more miles to go before you get to the park is often meaningless for them. For older children, you may want to make a very simple map graphic with a general outline of your route and simple pictures to represent landmarks and stops along the way. Give them a crayon or marker to trace the route as you travel, and cross out each destination as you reach it.

Although you cannot make the journey any shorter, there are some ways you can help your child pass the time.

- Prepare a special travel activity tote bag. Keep it stocked with simple games and activities that do not require many pieces or a lot of space. There are magnetic travel games that are designed just for this purpose. Do not forget to bring along your child's favorite music CDs or books on tape.
- Play "I am an animal." Each person pretends that he is an animal and he gives out clues for the others to guess what he is. For example, "Who am I? I am big, very big. However, I like to eat very, very small animals. I like to swim, but I am not a fish."
- For car travel: Have a scavenger hunt. Prepare a list of items in advance (cow, fence, gas station, yield sign). Everyone works to see how many items on the list she can spot.
- For car travel: Play "Everyone count." Each person is assigned an item to look out for and count. For example, you will count churches, Dad will count mailboxes, and your child will count flags.

Waiting for Attention

One of the most common situations that you are likely to witness is your child's impatience when he is demanding your attention. Maybe your child is constantly calling on you to watch him perform a stunt, or he wants you to play a game with him. Perhaps you find that every time you start a conversation with an adult, your child interrupts you. One mother shares, "It never fails. My children could be content and happily off playing somewhere, yet the minute I get on the phone, they need me. Whether they are quarreling amongst themselves or clinging to my legs, they manage to interrupt me almost every time with some problem that 'just can't wait.' If I try to reason with them, a temper tantrum erupts."

Frequent demands for attention and interruptions can be very tiresome and frustrating for you. There are, indeed, times when you must respond promptly to your child's calls for attention or help. It will be helpful for you to teach your child about what constitutes an emergency and what is of lower priority. After all, what you consider unimportant may seem urgent for the child at the time. Refer to the classic folktale The Boy Who Cried Wolf. Discuss possible situations, including real, everyday "emergencies" such as broken toys, spills, arguments, lost items, being hungry, or wanting the TV turned on. Try making a list with simple pictures arranged in order of importance. Make clear the distinction between a simple want and a real emergency such as the need for the potty, someone being hurt or in danger, or other issues of concern to you. Maybe even designate a special emergency signal such as a code word or whistle.

 Essential

When your child frequently interrupts you for nonemergencies, often your best course of action is to ignore her. Particularly if she is using outlandish behavior such as yelling, whining, or making silly or disturbing noises. Your response will just encourage the behavior.

When the situation does not qualify for emergency status, your child needs to learn to wait. It will be helpful to set up standards of behavior in advance. Be clear how you want her to act when she is waiting. You may want to establish a way that you can acknowledge her. A wink or a pat on the arm can say, "I know that you want my attention; I will be with you when I am finished." If your child often interrupts you while you are on the telephone, try having a special waiting activity basket that you can store nearby. Keep the basket filled with drawing paper, crayons, and table games that will interest and occupy your child. Let this be a special basket that is used just for waiting times.

Helping Your Child Take Turns

Potentially, the most difficult time for your child to be patient is when she is asked to wait her turn. Turn taking can be difficult not only because children have a hard time waiting, but also because they are often being asked to share. You can read more about helping your child with sharing in Chapter 7.

There are some ways that you can help your child remain patient during turn taking. Acknowledge and empathize with your child's feelings. You may say something like, "I know it is hard to wait for something that you want." Alternatively, you might say, "I see you are anxious to take your turn on the swing set. You will have your turn as soon as Mary is finished."

Point out examples of turn taking in everyday life. You can serve as a good role model: "We are stopped at the stop sign because I have to wait my turn to go." "There is a long line at the store because other people need their turn to pay for their food." Waiting for a turn does not mean your child must stand there and watch. Adding inactivity to waiting makes it more frustrating. Help your impatient child find something else to do until it is his turn: "While Nina is having her turn mixing the batter, why don't you help me grease the cookie sheet?" "While you are waiting for your turn on the bike, you can play with the basketball."

Question?

Should I time a turn?

When possible, allow each child to use the toy for as long as he wishes. By doing so, you show respect and prevent their frustration. They should not feel rushed and unable to complete their chosen activity. The exception would be if there is a restricted time span and limiting each child's time is the only way to grant each child a turn.

Waiting for Your Child

While your child's understanding of time is not developed, he will experience many frustrations. Waiting is difficult when time passes too slowly for him. There may also be times when time is moving too rapidly for him, and he is unprepared to adjust. Consequently, he will have difficulty with the change and transition. He may want you to wait for him!

Because your child's experience is grounded in the here and now, she may become very absorbed in an activity without foreseeing its conclusion. When you suddenly appear and announce that her time is over, she may be shocked and highly upset. Young children also often have a difficult time shifting gears. If they were engaged in a very active game such as chasing lightning bugs, it will be challenging for them to promptly stop and sit quietly while you read them a story. They will need time to cool down first.

Alert!

Each child is different. Your child may respond better to a visual warning that her time will be over soon. You can use an hourglass so that she can see the sand fall. If she responds better to auditory clues, use a ticking timer.

You can reduce your child's frustration simply by giving her fair warning. It will be particularly helpful if you can give her a concrete reference: "After you kick the ball two more times, it will be time for us to go home." "I am setting this alarm for three minutes. When the bell rings, it will be time to clean up your toys." It is okay if you feel that your child needs more than one warning. However, it is important that you follow through without extending the time. For example, you may say, "You have five more minutes to play before it is time to come inside." Then after three minutes, "Okay, finish your activity. Now there are only two minutes left before you need to come in." Avoid giving in to your child's repeated pleading for "just one more turn/minute."

CHAPTER 11

It's Too Hard:
Frustration Tantrums

Y our preschooler was excited to start building the model air-
plane kit his uncle gave him. However, fifteen minutes into
the project, he has pieces strewn all over the table and
he's forcefully trying to cram Tab C into Slot A43. He bursts into
tears and sweeps all the pieces to the floor. As he runs out of the
room, he yells, "I hate this stupid thing!" Why is your child so
easily frustrated? How can you help him tackle new skills calmly
and confidently?

Why Your Child Is Easily Frustrated

Frustration is a common experience for children. They are easily frustrated when things do not go their way. This also happens when they
feel that they do not have control over a situation, or a task becomes
too difficult for them. Daily activities and skills that you may take
for granted (walking, dressing) are all skills that must be learned.
Because you were very young when you learned these
skills, it is likely that you do not recall the setbacks and
challenges that you experienced while learning them.
More than likely, you fell on your bottom a few times
before you walked. You may have twisted many knots in
your shoelaces before you could tie them correctly.

 *Fact*

Almost all human behaviors are learned. The exceptions are the reflexes that we are born with. Behaviors that are innate and do not have to be learned include sneezing, yawning, and blinking.

The road to mastering many new skills is not smooth. In fact, challenge is necessary for learning. It motivates you to keep trying and it results in a sense of mastery and accomplishment when you succeed.

Frustration in Young Children

Temper tantrums that are caused by frustration usually peak between the ages of four and seven. However, you may see your younger child exhibit frustration while trying to complete a task. The main cause for frustration tantrums is often your toddler's lack of problem-solving ability.

If your toddler has difficulty seeing more than one possible solution to a problem, she will often just focus on one single way to reach her goal. For example, if your daughter sees that her favorite baby doll is perched on the top shelf of her bedroom closet, she might decide that the way to get the doll down is to knock it off the shelf by throwing another object at it. She picks up one of her shoes from the closet floor and takes aim at the baby doll. With all of her strength, she throws the shoe in the air, hoping it will knock the doll off the shelf. She is not strong enough or tall enough—the shoe barely reaches the clothing bar before it falls back to the floor. Your persistent daughter tries again and again. Each time she throws the shoe, it fails to reach the height of the top shelf. She continues until she becomes so frustrated that she either gives up or has a temper tantrum. At this age, she does not have the ability to analyze or reflect on why her strategy is not working. Furthermore, it will not occur to her that there are multiple potential solutions that she could try, such as using a broom handle to knock the baby doll down or simply calling on you for assistance.

Frustration in Older Children

As your child matures, he may begin to have more frustration temper tantrums. Your child is developing rapidly and acquiring many new skills. He is rapidly trying to acquire new skills that may include skipping, swimming, skating, bike riding, and participation in team sports. Once he enters school, there is a whole new demand for him to master academic and refined social skills as well. For your young school-aged child, skill achievement and competence become closely tied to his self-esteem. For example, your child may be aware of what reading group he is in and whether he is in the "slow" group. If he is always the last one picked for a sports team, he's sure to devalue his own abilities.

 Essential

Your child will not be good at everything, and there is no reason for you to expect him to be. Help your child find his niche. Maybe he is not very athletic but he plays the piano well. Once you discover his strengths, be sure to support and encourage him.

As children mature, they become more aware of their own competence or lack of competence. This is partly due to their heightened cognitive ability to reflect on their own accomplishment or failure. The younger child does not stop to think, "Did that turn out as I planned?" "What went wrong?" or "What can I try next time?"

As children get older, their social contacts and experiences start to expand. Your toddler's social world was probably limited to her immediate family, a few family friends, and, perhaps, day care peers. Now your school-age child has frequent contact with people at school, other children in the neighborhood, and, possibly, myriad other social opportunities such as scouting, camping, dance or music classes, and other community and recreational activities.

With these new relationships comes an increased exposure to evaluation from others. In school, your child's progress is frequently evaluated. Here your child is constantly receiving feedback, both formally (grades) and informally (notes home, classroom rewards), on his academic performance and competence.

Evaluation from others continues beyond the school walls. On the playground, your child is facing evaluation from her peers. Does she fit in? Will she be picked for a team? Both in and out of school, competition becomes important. Who is the fastest runner? Who will be chosen for the lead in the school play? Whose essay will be put up on the classroom bulletin board?

These evaluations are hard to avoid and force children to reflect on their own personal sense of competence and ability. When they feel that they do not measure up, they may be inclined to become frustrated. They may even become self-critical and feel inferior.

There is some good news. While school-aged children may indeed experience frustration as they try to master new abilities and skills, they simultaneously acquire the developmental maturity to cope with these frustrations. Their emotional maturity allows them to feel more secure than a younger child would when it comes to trying new things and taking risks, and their increased attention span allows them to persevere as they try to complete a new task or solve a problem. They are more likely to view failure as a setback or as a onetime event and will be more likely to attribute the failure to circumstances rather than perceived shortcomings. Consider the example of a child having a hard time learning to do a cartwheel. The younger child may think, "I won't ever be able to do this because I am a klutz." The older child may think, "I had a hard time doing a cartwheel today; maybe I need someone to show me how to keep my legs straight."

Give Opportunities for Success

It is important that your child has many chances to feel competent and successful. Each time your child succeeds, he gets a boost to his self-esteem and confidence. When your child feels confident about herself, she will be likely to persevere through future tasks with less frustration. These benefits of success are particularly true when the completed task was something perceived by your child as difficult or challenging. Think about it, did you feel a great sense of pride and accomplishment after you brushed your teeth this morning? Probably not. In comparison, recall how you felt after finally achieving a goal that at first seemed insurmountable to you. After conquering that dragon or climbing that mountain, you had a boost in confidence and other challenges did not seem as daunting.

When Your Child Does Not Feel Successful

Over time, continuing failure can weigh children down just as much as success lifts them up. When their efforts often result in failure, they may begin to develop self-doubt and feelings of inferiority. If these feelings persist, he may become withdrawn, and he may experience depression. After a while, your child's motivation to succeed, or even try, will falter. This is called learned helplessness.

Here are some signs your child is experiencing learned helplessness.

- She actively avoids activities or tasks that she perceives as challenging. She makes excuses like, "No, I don't want to learn how to ice skate. It looks boring to me."
- He becomes apathetic about tasks. You may hear him proclaim, "So what, I don't care that I failed that stupid test."
- She becomes negative about tasks. She may say something like, "Why should I even try that dance step? I know I won't be able to do it."

Set the Stage for Success

You can provide opportunities for your child to feel successful and competent. You can also guide her in making choices that will be appropriately challenging for her. For example, when you take her to the library, you can help her select a book that is suitable for her reading level. If she is reading at the fifth-grade level, you obviously wouldn't recommend picture books, but you'd also wait a few years before suggesting *War and Peace.* By guiding her choices, you can stop her from getting in over her head and becoming overwhelmed and frustrated.

Alert!

It is not possible for you to protect your child from failure completely. Some failure is inevitable and valuable. We all learn from our mistakes and trial and error. Through failure, we learn how to cope better the next time around. You learn that failure in one task does not mean future failure in similar tasks. You also learn that failure does not shape your worth as a person.

Select Toys and Materials Wisely

Your goal is to choose materials that match or slightly exceed your child's ability level. Be aware that toys that are well below your child's ability level are not challenging and may lead to boredom and frustration. To understand how this might happen, imagine giving a stacking-ring toy to an eight-year-old. His boredom may quickly escalate into irritation or frustration as he says, "This baby toy is no fun— it's stupid!" He then proceeds to use the rings as projectile weapons. Alternatively, imagine giving a fifty-piece puzzle to a two-year-old. Her frustration to match the shapes may quickly escalate, and she may begin to bend the pieces in half to make them fit.

Make the Environment Child Sized

You can reduce a lot of frustration by having child-sized equipment and furniture for your child's use. It is much less frustrating for a toddler to use her sippy cup than a ten-ounce tumbler. Additionally, imagine how much easier it would be for her to put toys away if she could reach the toy shelf. A child-sized environment will also help her become more independent, which will give her a feeling of competence.

Make Tasks Easier

You can reduce a lot of frustration for your child if you set up the routine tasks and self-help tasks in ways he can manage. You can make getting dressed easier for him. Find items that are pull-ons. Avoid complex lacing, buckles, and zippers. Your child can feel mastery over self-grooming tasks if you set up everything beforehand (toothpaste on the brush, comb laid out).

Responding to Frustration

By the way that you respond to your child when she is frustrated, you can help her cope with her strong feelings. You also have the opportunity to help her learn how to manage her frustration in the future. To effectively respond to your child's frustration, you need to be alert and in tune with her threshold for frustration. Each child is different. Some remain calm and persistent when challenged, and other children try something only once before becoming overwhelmed. By careful observation, you may also learn specific triggers for your child's frustration. Does he tend to become more frustrated when he is being evaluated? Does competition make him feel stress, and therefore make him less resilient to frustration? Additionally, consider if your child is more frustrated by certain tasks. Perhaps she can calmly tackle her math homework but she falls to pieces if she is trying to master a new dance step. Knowing your child's threshold and triggers will help you prevent some frustration for her and will help you respond with sensitivity when she is having difficulties.

 **Essential**

> With experience, you will learn when to intervene or respond when your child is frustrated. You may find that by responding quickly, you can prevent your child's frustrations from escalating. Alternatively, you may find that if you jump in too rapidly, your child may be resentful and resistant to your help. A good rule of thumb: the younger the child, the quicker your response should be.

Respond with Empathy

The most powerful thing you can do when your child is frustrated is to respond with empathy. Let your child know you hear and understand what he is feeling. You can be specific and show that you empathize by saying things such as, "Look at all those pieces! I can understand why this puzzle is driving you bonkers." Or, "I know this homework is challenging your ability to stay calm."

Responding with empathy helps to diffuse your child's strong feelings of aggravation or frustration. You show him that his feelings are acceptable and understandable. You are helping him gain the perspective that he is not alone in feeling this way. The knowledge that someone else can relate to this experience, and that it is okay to feel frustrated, because everyone gets frustrated at times, will be effective in helping your child manage his frustration.

Respond with Encouragement

Your response should be encouraging. Encouraging statements will help your child stay positive about tackling the current task. Encouraging statements also build your child's confidence, something she will need to be successful in the future. You can encourage your child by saying things like, "I have faith that you will be able to do it. I am confident you can find the answer." Or, "Your hard work will pay off."

When children (and adults) are frustrated, they often send themselves discouraging messages and develop their own internal negative voice. That voice sends messages such as, "This is too hard for me," "If I were not so dumb, I could do this," "I bet I will just fail again." If you continue to encourage your child, you will replace those negative messages with positive ones such as, "I know I can," and "I bet I will find the answer."

Help Your Child Tackle New Skills

When your child becomes frustrated while trying to complete a task, you have a great opportunity. Children do need help learning how to solve problems, and you can teach them how to manage their frustration when they are tackling new tasks. You can also help them to advance their cognitive and problem-solving abilities.

 **Essential**

When you observe that your child is becoming frustrated with a task, the first thing you should do is respond with empathy and encouragement. Your attempts to guide or teach her will be futile unless she is calm. This may include assisting her with the task after a cooldown period.

When Your Child Is Overwhelmed

Many times your child may be feeling overwhelmed by the size or complexity of the task. If this is the case, you will need to help him break the task into smaller pieces that are more manageable. Asking him to do a task that seems simple to you, such as cleaning his room, might cause him to break out in a frustration tantrum. If you make this request only to return twenty minutes later to find him walking around his messy room aimlessly with only a few items moved to different places but not put away, you know that this is a sign that he needs some help. Stop him and say, "I can see you are feeling frustrated and overwhelmed. I know you can do a good job once you get started."

You then help him break down the task into manageable pieces. Try to start with one thing at a time. If there are clothes strewn across the room, suggest that your child put away those first instead of getting him to put away his toys or put his books in order at the same time. By breaking down the task into more manageable pieces, your child will feel less overwhelmed and can try to use the experience as a model for what to do next time—and hopefully avoid the frustration that leads to a tantrum.

From Problem to Solution

Whether a task is large or small, simple or complex, your child may be frustrated, and you can help guide her. The first step is to identify the problem or behavior that is preventing your child from reaching a desired goal. Whenever possible, try to get your child to figure this out for herself. You can ask guiding/leading questions such as, "Why do you think this puzzle piece will not fit?" "Can you think of a reason why you spill the juice each time you try to pour it?"

 **Fact**

Your child will acquire many new skills simply by observing you. You can choose to intentionally model or demonstrate how to complete a task for your child before asking her to attempt it.

Help the child reflect on her failed attempts. Involve her in the generation of possible approaches or solutions. You could say, "How did you try to use this puzzle piece? What else could you try?" or "If you think the juice glass is too small, what could you try?"

If you believe the initial frustration is a result of a lack of your child's problem solving, you can then back away and let him try solutions. You will find more on helping your child with problem-solving skills in Chapter 18. If your child's abilities are at the root of the problem, you will probably need to model the solution or guide him through the process.

Approaching a Task Together

Children learn best by direct hands-on experience. You can start by involving them as a helper in a task. This can be something very simple. For example, "I am going to brush your teeth. Put your hand over mine and you can see how to use the brush." Or, "You can help me make your bed. Hold on to the corner of the sheet." Involve them increasingly as their competence grows. For example, next, you can hold on to one corner of the sheet while your child tucks in the corners. Eventually, you can let him do it on his own.

Independent Skill Advancement

When your child is attempting to complete a new task independently, you should remain available to help. Here you have the opportunity to do two things: You can assist your child in succeeding with her chosen task, and if she is successful, you can guide her to the next level of development.

Once you are familiar with where your child is with his skill development, you can give him support and guidance to move on to the next step of complexity. This is called scaffolding. During scaffolding, you serve as an external support for your child. You help identify the next level of skill and lead him to the next level of complexity. For example, when your child easily ties a slipknot in his shoelaces, you could say, "You can tie a slipknot, so now you can learn to make a bow. Do you know what the next step is? That is right, you need to have loops. Let's do one together." Or, if your child is in the swimming pool and comfortably floating while holding on to the kickboard, you might say, "Now that you can float using a kickboard, how do you think you can use it to move across the pool?"

When possible, use prompting to try to get your child to think and act independently. You can prompt her by using open-ended or leading questions: "What should you do?" "What else could you try?" Offer help only as it is needed. Offer less and less help as your child gains mastery and confidence.

By identifying your child's developmental progress and pinpointing their abilities, you will be able to guide them to the next level of competence. The table here lists some milestones in skill development and the approximate age range at which you can expect your child to accomplish them. They include self-help, motor, and cognitive skills.

Skills Milestones	
Age (in months)	**Skill Achieved**
12–16	Walks
14–17	Drops small object in narrow opening
15–18	Scribbles with crayon
16–20	Feeds self with spoon
17–26	Builds tower of four cubes
18–24	Kicks ball
18–24	Manages stairs if holding on to railing
24–36	Pedals tricycle
28–38	Threads large beads
38–40	Chops paper with scissors
40–48	Builds tower of ten cubes
40–48	Strings small beads
48–60	Ties shoes
48–60	Bounces and catches tennis ball

Preventing Frustration Tantrums

Although you cannot prevent all frustration temper tantrums, there are steps you can take to reduce them. To keep your young child safe, it's necessary to put restrictions on some of their activities and behavior. Toddlers struggling with their own autonomy will often feel frustrated with so many limits. Many times during a day, the typical toddler hears, "Stop doing that" or "Don't touch that." You can keep those necessary limits and reduce your child's frustration simply by limiting negative statements and putting a positive spin on your directives. Change those negative messages to, "I need you to put that down and come sit with me" and "You can play with this toy instead."

Set up your child for success, not failure. Look at your expectations for your child. Are they both age appropriate and on target for his capabilities? He will base his own sense of accomplishment and competence on how he perceives he measures up to your expectations. Avoid crafts that have a set pattern or model. Stay away from kits or paint-by-numbers sets. If you do crafts or projects with her, emphasize the process rather than the finished result. Instead of having her glue cutout shapes to make a kitty picture that looks like one in the craft book, why not give her a variety of supplies and encourage her to explore and create what she wishes? Some good examples of materials that focus on process rather than product include clay, finger paints, collage materials, and papier-mâché.

Alert!

Are you sending your child unintended messages that she does not or will never measure up to? Stop yourself before you say things like, "Why can't you be more like your big brother?" "I was always good at math, so what is your problem?" or "I'll be so embarrassed if you do not make the team."

It is okay to have positive expectations for your child. However, when she is young, focus on her effort and personal improvement rather than on her achievements. For example, "I can see how hard you are tying to snap your jacket" or "I see you are spending more time practicing your piano lessons." What counts here is not her accomplishment or skill but her effort. With your encouragement, she will keep trying.

CHAPTER 12

Look at Me: Attention Tantrums

Y ou may have heard that you should ignore your child's temper tantrums. That, after all, they are only fits that are staged either to manipulate you or to attract your attention. The truth is, many temper tantrums are a result of environmental, developmental, or maturity issues, and your child is not acting intentionally. However, as your child grows, she may learn that a temper tantrum and other behaviors such as whining are indeed effective ways to get what she wants.

The Need for Attention

Young children need and crave attention. They started their life as completely dependent beings. As they mature, they may need you less and less to meet their physical needs; however, they will depend heavily on you to meet their emotional needs. They will continue to need your attention for comfort, support, and validation through their childhood and adolescence.

The amount of attention your child needs will depend on his unique temperament and personality style. For example, your four-year-old may be constantly under your feet asking you to play with him, while another four-year-old is perfectly content to spend hours playing in her room alone. Children who need or crave attention are usually very active or outspoken about letting you know. Whether your child needs a lot or a little attention, they may go to great lengths if they feel they are not getting enough.

Whining for Attention

As your child grows, you will see an increase in attention-seeking behaviors. Some of these behaviors may be positive, such as becoming more affectionate or trying to be your little helper. However, your child may also adopt negative behaviors that he has learned, resulting in more attention from you. Some of these negative behaviors include tattling, swearing, bragging, and whining.

The Birth of Whining

Whining is a very common attention-seeking behavior in young children. By definition, whining is a verbal complaint, usually done in a wavering, drawn-out, high-pitched voice. Usually appearing in the preschool years, whining often lasts through adolescence. You may not recall when your child started to whine, but now you find it a common behavioral pattern that is difficult to break. Often it has its birth in a child's disappointment or frustration. In fact, whining may be a warning sign that a temper tantrum is close at hand.

Raise Her Awareness

It is quite possible that your child is unaware that she is whining. Even so, on an unconscious level, she has discovered that whining gets results. Consequently, your first step to curtail whining is to help your child become aware that she is whining. Let her know the moment she begins to whine. You may find it helps to show her what whining sounds like. It sounds very different to the listener. One father did this effectively by simply answering his daughter's whining with exaggerated whining of his own. "But Da-a-a-ddy," she would moan. "Ple-e-e-ase let me have a cookie." Then he would answer, "But Su-u-sie, you ca-a-a-n't have a cookie." She quickly found his whining irritating, and now that she was able to hear how she sounded, she stopped whining. Another idea is to tape-record your child when she whines. Also tape a sample of her regular speech tone, and play both recordings back for your child. Let her hear the difference!

End the Whining

Whining is a form of communication. If simply making your child aware of his whining does not make him stop, you need to help him to find better ways to communicate. Your best course of action is to be firm. Tell him that, from now on, he must use a normal voice. When he whines, remind him, "Use your normal voice. I will not listen to you when you are whining." Initially, your child may whine more. Stand firm. If you make it clear that you will not respond, he will soon give up whining for good. Remember, sometimes simply ignoring your child when he whines will quickly send the message that whining is not an effective way to communicate or get attention.

Is a Temper Tantrum Just for Attention?

Your child will learn how to get attention from you based on how you respond to his behavior. This is certainly true for temper tantrums, and indeed, he can learn to start tantrums to manipulate you for what he wants and to get attention from you.

Essential

Attention or manipulative temper tantrums usually will not appear until your child is four or five years old. Your younger child simply does not have the emotional and cognitive finesse to think, "Hmm, I really want this toy. I bet that if I were to scream and yell, Mom would give in and give me the toy." There is no premeditation or planning behind her temper tantrums.

There are many reasons why your child may have a temper tantrum. Conventional wisdom tells us that most, if not all, temper tantrums are intentionally designed by the child for manipulation and attention. In fact, this is not true. Not only are attention-seeking tantrums not as common as others, but you can learn how to respond in order to discourage your child from throwing them, thus decreasing their occurrence even more.

To determine whether your child is intentionally throwing an attention-seeking temper tantrum, ask yourself these questions. If your child is having an attention-seeking tantrum, you should be able to answer yes to at least one of these questions:

- Is my child's motive clear? Can I tell what my child has to gain by throwing this temper tantrum?
- Is the child demanding something? Am I being asked to give in?
- Is my child's emotional reaction less intense than it has been during other temper tantrums?
- Does my child seem to have control and intentional choice over his behavior?
- Does the intensity of the tantrum increase when an adult responds?

It is important to identify from the start whether your child is having a temper tantrum for attention or manipulation. With other types of tantrums, you will often need to be sympathetic, responsive, and comforting. In contrast, when coping with an attention-seeking tantrum, you will need to be firm and often even unresponsive.

Learning Through Imitation

There are two main ways that children learn specific behaviors: through reinforcement and through imitation. It is fortunate that they do not have to learn everything through reinforcement or direct experience. If a child sees that someone on television is injured after they perform a dangerous stunt, she can learn to avoid this behavior without trying it out. Your child can witness someone tripping on a loose rug on the floor. She knows that either she must be careful walking in the same place or she needs to fix the rug. A child does not have to also trip to know this, because she can learn just by seeing what happened to someone else. Rather than experiencing the consequences, she can observe someone else's and understand that the same behavior will result in the same consequences for her.

 **Fact**

A great deal of learning occurs through observation and imitation. Language, habits, social skills, and fears are just a few things that are commonly learned by imitation. Learning through imitation continues as we age, and it helps us acquire academic, musical, and athletic skills.

Your Child Is Watching

If your child's cousin picks up her toys and gets a reward from Grandma, your child will be motivated to pick up his toys in expectation that Grandma will give him a reward also. Like other behaviors, temper tantrums can be learned through imitation. For example, it is dinnertime and, without much warning, your two-year-old starts to squirm in his seat. When you gently try to encourage him to sit still and eat some of his peas, he starts to howl and he slides onto the floor like a blob of jelly. When he starts to kick your chair legs, you crouch down and pull him back to his seat. With a warm hug, you comfort him. "It's okay, honey. Do you not want peas? How about dessert? Are you ready for dessert?" This works wonders. Soon your two-year-old is happily munching on a peanut butter cookie, and all is well. Or is it? All the while, your four-year-old has been watching and thinking, "Hmmm, I would rather have a peanut butter cookie and all that attention rather than peas any day! I bet if I do what my brother did . . . "

Imitation in Action

In a now classic study, psychologist Albert Bandura examined the effect of observed consequences on learning. He took a group of four-year-old children and split them into three groups. Each group watched a film of an adult acting violently toward an inflatable punching doll. The first group of children saw a version of the film that showed the adult being praised and rewarded with treats for their aggressive behavior. The second group watched a film that showed the adult being yelled at for the aggressive behavior. In the third version, the adult was neither rewarded nor punished. Afterward, each child was given the chance to play with the doll that she saw in the video. There were children from all three groups who were then violent with the doll. However, children who saw the adult model rewarded were more likely to imitate the aggressive behavior. Conversely, the children who saw the film in which the adult was punished were less likely to imitate the behavior.

 Essential

Some children are more prone to be imitators. These children usually have low self-esteem and they are often doubtful of their own abilities and competence. Additionally, younger children are more likely to engage in imitation.

Four Steps of Learning Through Imitation

Learning through imitation comes naturally, but it is a complex process. There are four steps in learning through imitation.

1. **Attention.** The child must attend to the relevant behavior that resulted in the consequences.
2. **Retention.** The child must remember the behavior in order to replicate it when he wishes.
3. **Motor reproduction.** The child must be capable of completing the behavior that he wishes to imitate.
4. **Motivation.** The child must have a specific expectation of the consequences.

Further research has found that there is no difference in how a behavior is viewed. Children are just as likely to imitate a model regardless of whether it was a live person, a filmed person, or even a cartoon character. Such research highlights the strong impact that television and media violence can have on young children and their behavior.

Imitating You

Young children love to imitate their parents. Perhaps you have seen your little one mimicking how you talk, or you have seen her parading around in your high heels or dragging around your briefcase. Your child is most likely to imitate someone with authority whom he views as competent. He is also prone to imitate someone with whom he has a close and nurturing relationship. More than likely, this means you! For both good and bad behaviors, your child is closely observing you. Indeed, you serve as a powerful role model.

Just because you no longer writhe on the floor sobbing does not mean that you may not, on occasion, have a temper tantrum yourself. Even adults have times when, under stress or frustration, their nerves become frayed and they lose emotional control and composure. Here are some tips to tame your own temper:

- **Avoid known triggers.** If kids quarreling in the car drives you nuts, bring along a comedy tape or fun diversion. Better yet, see if you can trade off your car pool duty.
- **Be objective.** Put your emotions aside and focus on the facts. "She is pushing my buttons" becomes "She is screeching and it is hurting my ears."
- **Adjust your expectations.** Let go of perfection and roll with the punches.
- **Be nice to yourself.** Schedule a few minutes of your day to step back and relax. Even sitting down with a cup of tea for five minutes may help you regain composure.
- **Talk.** Find support with your spouse or a close friend.

You are not perfect. You are human and you will exhibit emotions. You cannot shelter your child from this at all times. However, it is wise to avoid losing emotional control in front of her. Be aware that if your child sees you yelling or crying at a time when you are out of control, she may find this upsetting. After all, she looks to you to be the one in charge and to help her maintain control. She is also looking to you to learn appropriate behavior.

Alert!

The well-known adage "Do as I say, not as I do" is not always effective. If your child imitates one of your negative behaviors and you subsequently punish her, she will be less likely to imitate your positive examples in the future.

If you have had a meltdown in your child's presence, do not pretend that nothing happened. Instead, take the opportunity to teach your child. You can say something like, "Whew, I was really angry at the neighbor. I lost my cool. I should not have yelled at her like that. The next time I am angry, I will come inside to calm down."

How Negative Attention Can Be Reinforcing

Are you rewarding your child's temper tantrums? Of course not. Well, at least not intentionally. However, it is possible that you will be reinforcing your child's behavior without realizing it. Children are fast learners; if they get what they want, even once, after having a temper tantrum, they will be sure to adopt this approach in the future.

You can easily see that giving in to your child's demands during a temper tantrum is reinforcing his behavior. Less obvious may be that you are reinforcing his behavior with attention. It is important to note that what you may consider negative attention may still be rewarding to your child, particularly if he feels he does not receive enough positive attention. Here are some direct and indirect responses that may actually be rewarding or reinforcing to your child.

- Making a big fuss over a minor misbehavior.
- Talking about your child's behavior when she can overhear you.
- Laughing at his behavior.
- Asking your child to repeat the behavior for your spouse to see.
- Spending a lot of time lecturing and discussing the behavior with your child.

 **Fact**

Do not expect yourself to change overnight as you try to acknowledge positive behaviors. Studies show that parents may ignore 90 percent or more of their child's positive behaviors. It will take your conscious effort and practice to learn to "catch" your child being good.

Your best defense is a good offense. Your child will be less likely to engage in behaviors such as temper tantrums for negative attention if he receives plenty of positive attention. Recognize and acknowledge your child when your child behaves as you wish. Do not be afraid to be direct: "I am glad that you put your socks away. I would like it if you could remember to do that every day." Additionally, do not discount the value of day-to-day loving times and interactions with your child, whether it is story time on a lap, popping popcorn, or just an extra hug.

Responding to the Attention Tantrum

When it comes to attention temper tantrums, your response will have a tremendous impact. In fact, your responses will either squelch or fuel your child's attention temper tantrums. Your child needs to learn that temper tantrums will not get her what she wishes, and that she will need to adopt appropriate behavior.

Do Not Give In

Rule number one: Do not give in. You may be determined to stand your ground, but there are times when your resolve may waver. You may be particularly challenged when you are tired, frustrated, stressed, or feeling guilty. Unfortunately, once you give in, all of the other times that you did not will be forgotten by your child. Consistency is crucial.

There are many reasons why you should not give in. First and foremost, you are rewarding your child for having a tantrum. When you give in, you give up power and authority. This may be upsetting to the child who counts on you for boundaries and guidance. You are not helping your child learn. When you give in, you take away the opportunity for your child to learn to manage her frustration independently. Sooner or later, you will not be there to provide what your child wants or to jump in to solve her problem. It may sound harsh, but your child does need to have experience in not getting her own way so she knows how to deal with it.

 Essential

Be on guard for times when you may be more likely to give in. Is your resolve shaken when your child is whining or screaming? Is mealtime or bedtime particularly trying? Perhaps you are more likely to give in when the temper tantrum occurs in public or you are worried that other people are judging your parenting ability.

What to Say

Briefly acknowledge your child when she is clearly throwing an attention temper tantrum. Show that you understand what she is feeling as you set the limit: "I know that you want a cookie, but it is too close to dinnertime." "I can see that you are mad, but you have to stay with Grandma today."

Clearly inform your child what the consequences will be. Let him know that he will not get what he wants and you will not continue to respond to his behavior. Do not allow your child to pull you into an argument. If he keeps whining or insisting, "But why? Oh, please!" simply restate your expectations. "I will not discuss this with you until you are calm." End the conversation by saying, "Let me know when you are done having a temper tantrum. Let me know when you are ready to be calm."

What to Do

Ensure that your child is safe. Clear away any hazards if she is thrashing about. You may need to stand close by to keep her safe and to let her know that you will be available when the temper tantrum is over. Next, stop responding to her behavior. Do your best to ignore her. Yes, this may be difficult. At first, her demands may escalate as she tries to get a reaction from you. Stand your ground. Do not speak to her, touch her, or look directly at her. Some parents will pretend to be engaged in other activities, such as listening to music, reading, or folding laundry. One mother shares:

> My son would have horrible tantrums. He would kick and scream and my insides would churn, ready to explode. One day, I found my husband's earplugs from work. I put them in; it was heaven. I could see my son and know that he was okay but the sound didn't drive me batty. I love it. Whenever I feel like I can't cope with the sound of a tantrum, I hunt down the earplugs. What I have learned is that my lack of reaction usually results in the tantrum's diminishing.

Alert!

You may be able to respond calmly with your child when he is having a temper tantrum that is caused by temperament or developmental growth. However, you may not find it as easy to be patient when you feel that he is intentionally staging a tantrum for attention or to manipulate you in some way. It is still important that you keep your composure and remain objective.

Eventually, your child will recognize that the tantrum is not producing the results that he was hoping for and he will stop. When he indicates that he is calm and in control, you can respond to him once again. Treat the end of a temper tantrum very matter-of-factly. Resist the temptation to lecture, warn, or moralize. If you make a big fuss now, you may still inadvertently reinforce his temper tantrum.

CHAPTER 13

Nobody Likes Me: Social Tantrums

Your six-year-old son does not want to go to school again. This is the third time this month. He claims he has a stomachache, but you suspect a different reason. He has been complaining that the other boys are teasing him about his new glasses. Your four-year-old daughter has just come running into the front yard. She is in tears and sobs, "Mary and Julie won't let me play with them!" How can you help your child? How can you smooth the road to better social relations for him or her?

The Importance of the Peer Group

The popular expression "no man is an island" is based in truth. We are inherently social beings, relying on others for companionship, emotional support, and in many cases, our very survival. From the start, your young infant is ready to engage in social interaction. She is responsive and expressive with other people almost immediately. As your child grows, her social circle will expand. Soon her relationship with you will be less prominent. Her relationships with children her own age will become most important.

The Value of Friends

Social interactions and friendships with others his own age will meet many of your child's critical psychological needs. When your child has at least one close friend, he will reap many benefits, including:

- A companion for fun and recreation
- A feeling of acceptance and positive self-esteem
- A supportive context for self-exploration and identity formation
- A base of stability during stress and transition

Your child's peer group interactions are valuable to his development. Interacting with other children will aid in his success both in school and later in the workforce. Within his friendships, your child will learn group problem-solving skills. He will learn how to manage both cooperation and competition. Your child may be more prone to temper tantrums if he does not feel accepted by his peer group. Close friendships will also boost your child's confidence; he will be more inclined to take chances or try something new.

 **Fact**

Studies show that aggressive children tend to associate with other children who have poor social skills. This can put them at a great disadvantage because they will not have as many opportunities for positive interactions or to learn prosocial skills from other peers.

Not all friendships may have a positive impact on your child. Peer pressure can be either a positive or a negative influence. Either way, peer pressure is a strong force that motivates your child to conform to the behavior of other children. Your child may neglect previously important hobbies or activities, or may even choose to do things that are personally or socially unacceptable. Personally unacceptable behavior is when you see your child make a dramatic shift in personal values, habits, or behavior. Your once-studious son is now spending homework time at the arcade. Or your prim and feminine daughter is now dressing sloppily and using curse words. You can influence your child's choice of peer group by fostering her friendships with children who offer a more positive influence, encouraging visits or taking them to an event. Try to provide social opportunities, such as sporting or hobby groups, that will allow your child to develop a peer network outside her school class group.

You can help your child resist peer pressure. Encourage him to be assertive, and promote his self-esteem. Discuss potential problems before they arise. For example, do not wait until you discover he is doing poorly in school before speaking to him about the value of homework. You may wish to role-play scenarios with your child. What will he do if someone pressures him to do something that he doesn't feel comfortable doing? What can he say if he is ridiculed for not conforming to his friend's behavior? You can also use news media and TV shows as an opportunity to discuss these issues. As you watch, you can ask questions like, "Do you think that is wise?" or "What would be the consequences of that choice?"

If your child seems reluctant to communicate about these issues, you could ask a trusted family friend or perhaps an older teen to discuss them with him.

Feeling Left Out

Psychologist Abraham Maslow identified the needs for affiliation and belonging as strong psychological drives. If your child is often feeling left out and rejected by her friends, she is likely to feel sad, angry, or even betrayed. In addition to temper tantrums, she is also at an increased risk for depression, anxiety, and low self-esteem.

Being a Part of the Group

Even a very popular child may experience times when he feels left out or rejected by his friends. For most children, this is an infrequent event, but for other children, it can become a persistent and troublesome issue that causes them considerable distress or anguish. These children require assistance joining or staying in a peer group. You may need to model how to do this, or directly guide them. You may say something to them such as, "Come with me. Let's go ask Mark if you can help him build with the Legos." Or you can try to suggest a strategy for your child: "I can see that you are sad because Gina and Marla are playing house without you. Perhaps you can knock on the door and ask if you can be their babysitter?"

Alert!

The most common example of a child being snubbed or left out occurs within sibling relationships. Older children often will reject or avoid the younger sibling, regarding her as a pest or a tagalong. Forcing your older child to include the younger child will surely promote feelings of hostility. Be sure your younger child has plenty of opportunities to play with children her own age.

In addition to your child's having temper tantrums or directly complaining, there are signs that may indicate to you that your child is frequently being left out or rejected by his siblings or friends. By recognizing these signs, you may be able to intervene before your child becomes too upset.

- Your child receives fewer phone calls or invitations than his peers.
- Your child names casual acquaintances as close friends.
- Your child now has friends who are significantly younger or older than she is.
- Your child often returns home early from social events.
- Your child makes excuses to avoid social events.

The Sensitive Child

Your child's temperament may determine how resilient he is when he feels left out. Moreover, if your child is overly sensitive, he will be more likely to have difficulties. Additionally, your slow to warm up, shy child may need additional time to approach other children and make friends. Your child may not feel comfortable around other people until he has met them a few times. Your child may need you to directly introduce him to another child or he will wait until the other child makes the first move.

Each child reacts differently to being snubbed or left out. The key is how she explains the event. Some children will blame themselves: "There must be something wrong with me." "If only I were not so fat." These children suffer from poor self-esteem and will be inclined to withdraw from social situations. Some children will blame others: "Children in this town are mean." "I bet they like hiding from me." These children often react with anger and aggression. On the other hand, socially competent children are more likely to blame circumstances: "I bet they would have invited me if there were more room in the car." Alternatively, they recognize the situation can be controlled or changed by their behavior: "Next time, I will remember to ask to come along, instead of assuming I will be invited." If your child is blaming herself or others, you can step in and offer the other perspective. If your child says, "Susie does not like me anymore. She did not invite me to go to the amusement park with her family!" You might say, "There could be many reasons why Susie did not invite you. It seems to me that she does like you; I wonder if maybe her family did not allow her to invite you."

Why Children Feel Rejected

There are many reasons why your child is feeling left out or rejected. Younger children are often very fickle. Their friendships are usually based on superficial reasons (who lives close by or who has the trendiest toy) and are often short lived. Preschool-aged children often say things like, "I won't be your friend if you don't give me some of your candy" or "I'm not inviting you to my party because you did not sit with me at lunchtime." Consequently, friendship preferences change frequently. Your child may be extremely upset when a peer or classmate does not call him a friend. He is still trying to master emotional control as well as social skills. A simple occurrence, such as a classmate's not picking him as a partner for a game, may be enough to trigger a temper tantrum. Fortunately, young children do not hold grudges, and hurt feelings are often quickly mended.

Transitions may also make peer relationships more difficult. Moving or changing schools are two examples of times that may be trying for your child even if she is not especially sensitive to feelings of loss or rejection. All change is stressful for a young child. Losing a friend can be particularly upsetting, especially if this was your child's closest relationship and her friend was a confidant.

Popularity

There is tremendous value put on being popular. Children and adults alike desire to be well liked and to be a part of the "in crowd." Being popular means you belong and are accepted. It means you are picked for teams, invited to parties, and are rarely left behind.

Being popular is not an all-or-nothing status. In fact, most children will fall somewhere in between. If your child is part of the in crowd, she is in the minority. Only about 30 percent of children fall into this category. As many as 50 percent of all children are in the middle of this social hierarchy. Though not widely popular, these children have a small circle of close friends.

 *Fact*

Even if your child has only one friend, this is often sufficient for him to feel confident and accepted. Only about 10 percent are children who truly have no friends.

What Makes a Child Popular?

Children make quick judgments about their peers. There are particular traits they look for when choosing friends. To help your child become more popular, consider some attributes other children want to have in their friends: The popular child is fun to be around. His disposition is generally upbeat and positive. The popular child is seen as honest and trustworthy. The popular child is confident and approachable. The popular child is empathetic and supportive. Although some of these traits are innate, others such as honesty and empathy can be developed.

What Makes a Child Unpopular?

Even if your child possesses the above traits, there may be times when she is rejected by her peers. Sometimes the basis for this can be quite arbitrary. Your child may be unpopular simply because of what side of the street she lives on or what brand of sports shoes she is wearing. Physical differences also can lead to your child's being rejected. Unfortunately, children do reject other children based on physical attributes, and your child may be teased or rejected because of various physical traits, including weight, stature, or facial features. One mother shares an example: "One morning I found my son having a fit in the bathroom. He was out of control, sobbing and shaking. He had a pile of magic markers in the sink and he was trying to color black marker over his beautiful red hair! When I went to calm him down, he told me that he could not go back to day care. The reason? The other children told him that they would not play with him because they said that his red hair would burn them."

You can take steps to help your child feel positive about his physical differences. There are many wonderful children's books on this issue. One book in particular that you may want to check out is *People,* written by Peter Spier. This book looks at how people can be different in many ways (foods they eat, clothing they wear), but it ultimately focuses on how much everyone has in common. Perhaps you can tell your child about other famous people who share whatever unique quality is setting him apart. For example, the list of famous male redheads includes Woody Allen, Boris Becker, President Eisenhower, and Ron Howard.

Some behaviors will often cause a child to be unpopular. If your child is very withdrawn and shy, it is unlikely other children will make the extra effort to include her. Other children may even view your child as snobby or stuck-up. Your child is more likely to be unpopular if other children find her too aggressive or confrontational. Children are attracted to other children who are outgoing and approachable, but they will avoid a child who forces herself on others.

Essential

Boys and girls have different criteria for what makes someone popular. Popularity for girls is often based on looks and personality whereas boys assess popularity based on size, athletic competence, or sense of humor.

Additionally, your child will have difficulties if he has poor social skills. If he is impulsive, impatient, or lacking in listening skills, he may be disliked by other children. Unpopular children also often misinterpret the motives or intentions of other children. They may seem paranoid or view a friendly overture as insincere. This frequently results in behavior that is viewed as erratic or overly sensitive.

Ironically, how your child responds to being rejected can affect her popularity. When your school-age child cries or has a temper tantrum around other children, it is likely she will be labeled as a spoiled brat or a crybaby and will be further ostracized.

Understanding Cliques

Cliques or exclusive peer groups are rarely a positive socialization force for children. Being in a clique promotes feelings of affiliation and validation. However, often the largest impact of cliques is on those outsiders who either are denied entry or are actively victimized by clique members. Girl cliques, in particular, may use teasing and gossip as a means of reinforcing their own superiority or excluding others. Gossip is a common way for girls to reinforce their own social status while degrading someone else's. The root of a child's having a reputation or being labeled ("teacher's pet," "geek") is gossip.

A clique is a small peer group that has specific characteristics:

- Cliques are exclusive groups. Membership is restricted to a very few children.
- There is one child who is usually the leader or "queen bee." This child sets the norm for behavior within the group.
- Conformity is important. The clique will often have very narrow and defined codes for everything from socialization to fashion.
- Members of the clique usually have a general attitude of superiority toward those who are not in the clique.

If you see your child being snubbed by a clique, there are ways you can help her cope. Be sure to recognize what is special and unique about your child and help her celebrate it. Encourage her individuality. You can also help her find another avenue for affiliation (scouting, dance class). If your child is being directly victimized, use the strategies discussed in the next section on responding to bullies.

When Your Child Is Bullied

If your child is exposed to repeated systematic attacks from another child, he is being bullied. It is estimated that as many as 20 percent of all children are victimized by bullies. Most bullying occurs at the middle school level. Bullying behavior may include any of the following:

- Physical assault
- Taunts and name-calling
- Racial or ethnic slurs
- Threats or intimidation
- Extortion or stealing of money or possessions

Recent news of school violence has highlighted the pain and anguish bullies cause. If your child is being bullied, it is likely that he will feel fearful and vulnerable and have lowered self-esteem. He is at higher risk for depression and even suicide. Just the sight of a bully may cause your child to lose emotional control. The old adage "Sticks and stones may break my bones, but names will never hurt me" is just not true. Insults, taunts, and verbal intimidation can crush your child's spirit just as effectively as physical violence can.

Who Is Involved?

Bullies pick easy targets. Your child is more likely to be victimized if she is passive or submissive. The hallmark of a bullying relationship is the inequity of power. The bully is dominant and exerts physical or social power over his victim. If your child is socially awkward or a loner, he is at risk of being bullied.

 **Essential**

Although there are both male and female bullies, boys are in the majority. Boys tend to use physical aggression and intimidation. Girl bullies usually rely on subtler means such as teasing or social snubbing.

It was once believed that bullies were socially inept children with very low self-esteem. They were bullies, the old theory said, in order to raise their own self-esteem and confidence by putting down other children. It is now known that most bullies are usually confident and have a moderate or high self-esteem. Rather, bullying behavior seems to come from the child's temperament. Bullies tend to lack empathy and communication skills. They are often raised in a home where aggression is an acceptable method of conflict resolution.

Helping Your Child Cope with a Bully

You may or may not know if your child is having problems with a bully. Maybe your child is throwing a temper tantrum every morning, refusing to go to school because he is afraid of a bully. Maybe he asks you to give him a ride to school so he can avoid a bully down the street. It is important to know that many children do not report being bullied. They may not tell an adult due to shame, fear of retaliation, or the belief that the adult will be powerless to help them.

If your child does confide in you, it is imperative that you listen and do not discount her feelings or concerns. Reassure your child that she is not at fault. You can help your child avoid being bullied by becoming an unfavorable target. Bullies will go after loners. If your child stays with a group of friends, she will be less vulnerable. If your child has few friends, consider enlisting the help of an older sibling or neighbor for a while. Bullies mainly avoid targeting children who are not challenged or intimidated by the bully; therefore, your child needs to learn to be assertive and defend her own rights.

With role-playing and practice, you can directly teach your child how to be more assertive. For example, what would your child do if a bully demanded lunch money from him? A passive response is for him to meekly give up his money. An aggressive response is hitting the bully or trying to get money from the bully instead. An assertive response is calmly and firmly telling the bully no and walking away.

Have your child practice saying no to various scenarios like the one above. Your child is being assertive when he is defending his own rights or needs without harming someone else.

You can instruct your child that there are times when it is wise to ignore occasional teasing. The bully may find your child's emotional outburst and tears reinforcing. An emotional response is often what he is hoping for. On the other hand, if the teasing becomes persistent or if physical violence becomes a threat or reality, insist that your child seek help from an adult.

If You Need to Intervene

Although you may desire that your child will learn to solve problems independently, you need to draw the line when your child's emotional or physical health is in danger. If you choose to intervene, it is best to address the bully and your child separately before trying to bring them together peacefully.

If your child is being bullied at school, do not hesitate to contact school authorities. Schools take bullying very seriously. You should expect the school to work with you to resolve the problem. Many schools now have specific antibullying and antiharassment policies and programs in place.

Consider approaching the bully's parents only as a last resort. You may find them very apologetic and eager to resolve the matter. However, you may also find defiant or aggressive parents who are not willing to hear anything negative about their little angel.

Focusing on Fairness

It's not fair! This is a common complaint from young children. Your child may become disappointed, jealous, or angry when he feels something is not fair. In social settings, your child is apt to measure and compare possessions or privileges with his friends or siblings. He may say things similar to, "But Dilaika's mom allows her to . . . ," "I never get a turn to sit by the window," "You like my brother better than me!"

Young children, in particular, are very aware of issues of fairness or equity. Before the age of seven, your child will most likely be very rigid in her thinking. To her, everything is absolute. There are no gray areas in her reality. People are either good or bad. This leads to your child's expecting complete equity. They believe everyone should have the same bedtime, get the same number of cookies, and so on.

Of course, life does not work this way. When situations arise and it is clear there cannot be equality, the young, egocentric child will believe the privilege should belong to him. Such situations could include when only one child can be a line leader.

 **Fact**

Issues about fairness and equity are common among siblings. In fact, your children are more likely to quarrel, compete, and fight with siblings than with their same-aged friends. The positive news is that they are also more likely to cooperate with and show compassion to their siblings.

Your child's beliefs about what is fair are also tied to what she feels she is entitled to or deserves. These expectations are based on previous experiences, promises from adults, and comparing herself with other children. Does she see herself as well behaved and more deserving? Have you or another caregiver favored her in the past? You can help moderate your child's vigilance for fairness by helping her see the difference between "fair" and "equal." As a parent, you may strive to treat each of your children fairly, but rarely can you treat them equally. Giving each child the amount of food he needs to be satisfied and healthy is fair, but portions may not be equal. Asking each child to do chores is fair, but the amount of work may not be equal. So, the next time your child says, "It's not fair," you can explain why inequality can sometimes be fair.

Promoting Your Child's Social Skills

As your child grows, friendships will play an increasingly important role in her life. Some children seem to be naturally adept at making friends whereas others experience difficulty relating to other children. There are specific social skills your child can learn that will help him begin and maintain positive relationships, thus reducing social temper tantrums.

From Another Perspective

The ability to see someone's perspective is an important skill. Chapter 7 discusses how this ability develops and how children can learn to share. The ability to see someone else's point of view helps your child develop empathy and will aid him or her in conflict resolution. You can begin helping children with this skill by pointing out how other people may be feeling in a certain situation: "How do you think Lisa feels when you grab the ball away from her? I bet she is angry."

Another social skill is having an awareness of other children's emotional states and being able to interpret and predict their motivation and behavior. Children who pay attention to the body language and facial expressions of others will do well. With practice, your child can learn to be more in tune to others and adapt her behavior accordingly. You can model this behavior for your child: "Oh, Susie looks angry. This would probably not be a good time to ask her for a favor." "Trevor always seems to be grumpy in the morning. I will wait until later before I call him."

Cooperation

The ability to think as a team member will help your child with many social interactions, and she will tend to use more inclusive language, focusing on "we" rather than "I": "What do you think we should do today?" rather than "I want to go swimming now." Cooperation is an essential part of thinking as a team member. You can help your child by providing toys that can be used by more than one child at a time or playing games that focus on cooperation rather than competition. You can modify competitive games such as musical chairs. Instead of fighting for the remaining chairs, each time the music stops have children work together to see how many children can share the remaining chairs. No children are eliminated in this version. Cooperative games do not result in exclusion or hurt feelings.

The best way to help your child develop social skills is to give him many opportunities to interact with his peers. Make a point to get to know other families in the neighborhood, and invite families with young children over for a play date. Consider joining a Mommy and Me or play group where your child can have a chance to interact with other children in a small-group setting.

Essential

Show your child you value his friendships. Take the time to get to know your child's friends. Whenever possible, welcome your child's friends into your home and broadcast warmth and acceptance when they call or visit.

Conflict Resolution

You can help your child's burgeoning social skills by assisting her in managing conflict. Unless a physical confrontation is imminent, it is often best to stand back and encourage your child to solve the conflict on her own. A good rule of thumb is, the older the children are, the less you should need to intervene. Toddlers and young preschool-aged children will benefit from your guidance the most. Avoid jumping in and mandating a solution. Follow these four steps to guide young children in conflict resolution:

- Help identify the problem.
- Help them express their feelings.
- Encourage them to generate solutions.
- Lastly, help them agree and act on a solution.

Here is an example of how to use those steps in a real-life situation. You find that Jimmy and Tina are fighting over a bicycle. "I see that both of you want to ride the bike at the same time. Tina, how do you feel when Jimmy has the bike a long time? Jimmy, how do you feel when you know Tina wants to ride the bike? Do you have any ideas how we can make this fair?" "Tina has the idea that each of you can ride the bike two times around the yard before changing turns. Does that feel fair to you, Jimmy?"

CHAPTER 14

You Can't Make Me: Testing Tantrums

Y ou made it through the toddler and preschool years with your child. Yes, there were some tantrums, but happily, your child's emotional outbursts seemed to settle down when she entered school. Now, as your child is eight or nine or ten, you are seeing those outbursts return. You discover that many of the triggers are the same as they were before. Again, your child is struggling to find her identity and assert her independence. The difference is, instead of crying and throwing things, she is now slamming doors, talking back to you, and verbally challenging your authority. What can you do to restore the peace between you and your child?

Is Your Child Testing the Limits?

As your child matures, you may see that he is testing your limits and authority more than before. This can be a result of his cognitive and emotional growth. The way he sees and interacts with you will change. Your authority may no longer be as secure as it once was.

A New Perspective

Your older child is starting to see you in a new light. As he begins to strive to define his individual identity, he is compelled to further separate from you. Consequently, he may begin to view you as a fully human individual. He may become acutely aware of your weaknesses and faults. One teen reflects, "I always looked up to my dad.

When I was little, I saw him to be the smartest and strongest man in the world. He was always in control and could do anything. When I was older, this idealized image of him started to crumble. I came to him with my math homework and he was not able to help me. Maybe it was not the first time I saw he could not do something, but it was then that I realized that he was fallible. There was a time afterward when I felt disillusioned and I lost some respect for him." No longer does your child put you on a pedestal. When he first looks you in the eyes and sees you as a real person, it may take a while for him to like and respect what he sees.

Essential

Parents tend to spend less time with their older children than with younger children. Studies show, however, that parents are spending more quality time with their older children, even if it's limited. When older children and parents are together, they are more likely to be doing something interactive.

Another reason your child may seem more contrary and less respectful could be due to her improved cognitive abilities. Both experience and school lessons have promoted her critical thinking skills. In school, she no longer blindly accepts the answer. She has learned to compare and contrast differing viewpoints and facts before drawing her own conclusion. At home, this may mean she begins to question your authority. She may go as far as to ask for proof or justification for your opinions or rules.

Your child's social circle is expanding. As he enters school and makes more friends, the standards of the peer group become a predominant force in his personality and attitude development. Although he still loves you and is at least somewhat dependent on you, you will witness a change in his allegiance. Now, his decisions and actions will be influenced more by his desire to fit in and be accepted by his friends than to please you. Peer pressure can be a powerful force.

Other Factors

There are other factors that may contribute to conflict as they change your relationship with your child. Family dynamics and style shape interactions as your child matures. If there is already conflict present between other members of the family, tension may also increase with your child. For example, if there is marital discord, conflict may spill over to other family members. Over time, the way you interpret and respond to your child's behavior may increase conflict. This is particularly true if you have a tendency to attribute your child's behavior to negative personality traits or motivation. For example, "I believe you meant to hurt your little brother" or "I don't think you studied for that test; you failed because you are lazy." If you see things this way, you are likely to be more adversarial when you interact with your child. Additionally, your child may be aware of how you perceive him and may become defensive.

If your parenting style is coercive or very strict, your child will be more likely to challenge your authority. Rebellion is often her response, and she will try to break free from your control and forge her own identity and independence.

The Road to Independence

A predominant emotional task for your older child is his struggle for independence. For some, the road to independence is not smooth and can lead to your child's losing emotional control and displaying tantrum behaviors along with pouting or arguing.

Studies show a relationship between independence and parental conflict. In the early childhood years, the child is highly dependent on his parents and overall conflict or rebellion is low. During late childhood and into adolescence, when the child is making a bid for independence, conflicts with parents increase.

Conflict and rebellion decrease only when the child has become an independent young adult.

Fact

Contrary to common belief, most younger children who test limits will not undertake a full rebellion against their parents later on. Although most children will challenge their parents' authority from time to time, less than 20 percent of them will show complete rejection of their parents' guidelines and authority.

Stuck in the Middle

Your child is entering a time of major transition. He is no longer a little kid and yet clearly he is not fully an adult. This is truly a time of in-between, as much as toddlerhood was. In fact, you may find many similarities. Both groups are in a developmental transition. They are both striving for independence and want to be considered part of the older group. Conversely, both still want and need the securities associated with being in the younger group.

Still a Child

Your child is still quite dependent on you for shelter, food, and emotional support. For the most part, she is still enjoying many of the freedoms and privileges of being a child. She is free from adult responsibilities such as job, taxes, insurance, and bills. She still relies on you to care for her when she is ill, to resolve her conflicts, and to do her laundry. She also comes under your authority and has to conform to external requirements—from parents, school, and peers—not yet having the autonomy to make her own choices.

Society is now expecting your older child to display more emotional maturity and control. He is gaining valuable experience and skills that he will need to achieve independence and become an adult.

Alert!

Today's youth receives mixed messages about when one becomes an adult. After all, she may be allowed to date at fifteen, considered responsible enough to drive at age sixteen, and be old enough to vote at age eighteen. On the other hand, she must wait until she is twenty-one before she can legally drink alcohol. Expectations of "being an adult" with both privileges and responsibilities vary and can be conflicting.

Along with striving to be independent, your older child is beginning to define his own identity. The search for identity will lead him to reflect on questions like, "Who am I?" and "Where will I fit in?" There are many types of identities that your child may be exploring at this time.

Responsibility Leads to Independence

Just as it was with your toddler, your older child's struggle for independence may result in conflict and temper tantrum behavior. Your can reduce some conflict and power struggles. By giving your child increased responsibility, you can promote her feelings of independence and confidence. You can support your child's quest for independence with encouragement. Here are some sample statements that will show your faith in her new capabilities:

- I bet you can handle that.
- I know you will do what is right.
- It is clear you will make a good choice.

You will still have to enforce limits, but within those boundaries you can now allow her more freedom and choice. For example, rather than mandating exactly which household chores she will do and when, you turn the responsibility over to her. If you used to tell her, "You must vacuum the family room before you can play," now you can say, "Here is a list of possible chores that need to be done. I want you to choose three chores from this list to complete by the weekend."

Alert!

When you give your child added freedom of choice and responsibilities, you are letting go of some control. This does not mean you are withdrawing your support or interest. You may give him more choice and freedom, but you still monitor and remain involved with his progress.

Giving your child more control and independence helps him to learn to take responsibility for his own actions. Not all of his choices will be good ones, and you need to accept that. Unless your child will be hurt, it is important that you begin to step back and allow him to experience the consequences of the choices he has made. Perhaps you let him decide not to complete three household chores before the weekend. When Friday arrives, he is not allowed to go to a party, because he did not complete his responsibilities. Alternately, he has chosen to spend his money on a new CD, and then two days later he asks you for more money so he can buy a birthday present for his friend. Resist the urge to rescue him. By doing so, you usurp his responsibility and negate the value of this life lesson. This isn't easy, and often you'll find yourself emotionally torn, as it is a parent's natural urge to solve her child's problems. However, you need to be resolute and consistent. Remind yourself that the short-term pain will bring long-term gain.

The Older Child's Emotional Control

Your child has come a long way from the emotionally volatile and cognitively limited toddler or preschooler he once was. Your older child now has abilities that can help him regulate and control his emotions. You can help him utilize these strengths when temper tantrums loom on the horizon.

A Better Understanding

Your child now has a better understanding of her own emotions. She is able to pinpoint events or triggers that will feel a certain way. For example, she knows that when she visits her aunt Julia, she will feel happy and relaxed while she is visiting. In addition, she can predict that she will feel anxious when she has to give a presentation in social studies. The ability to predict emotions can enable her to avoid or modify circumstances she knows have the potential to lead to an emotional outburst or tantrum. You can help her learn to utilize these skills by gently prompting or reminding her, "Are you sure you want to invite Amber to your birthday party? Don't you recall, she always ends up upsetting you?" or "I know you often get cranky when we have to go shopping. Can you think of some way to make the trip easier for you?"

 **Fact**

Your older child is now developing social cognition. This is the ability to be aware of people's underlying motives and feelings. This allows him to see how someone else's personality will affect his behavior. By understanding and predicting the behavior of others, social interactions will not have as much conflict.

Less Egocentric

Your older child is no longer egocentric. In other words, he can truly see and understand the perspective of other people. He understands that the way his friends will respond and interact with him will be based largely on the way he displays emotion. He is now able to predict how they will react, too. For example, he knows that if he is overly aggressive, his friends will avoid or reject him. He can antici-pate that if he throws a tantrum while playing a game, his friends may ridicule him. He is now ready to make conscious decisions to suppress the way he displays undesirable emotions and behavior, including tantrums.

Verbal Outbursts

As your child ages, he may exhibit his loss of emotional control by verbally lashing out at you. He may become defiant or may challenge your rules or guidance. This behavior can be very upsetting to you. You want to discourage this behavior and encourage compliance and appropriate interaction.

When your child talks back, take a moment to consider your response. Keep your own composure. You may be stunned the first time your child sasses you. Many back-talk statements such as "you can't make me" or the now popular "whatever" seem to be designed just to push your buttons. When your child is outright defiant and challenging, it will take some restraint from you not to respond with anger. Avoid taking the bait and allowing yourself to be dragged into a power struggle.

Essential

Decide ahead of time where you wish to draw the line with back talk. Make it clear that it is not acceptable for your child to speak to you in that manner. You can respond by saying, "I think you can find a bet-ter way of saying that. I cannot help you until you speak nicely."

To keep a calm sense of perspective, recognize that your child is bound to have some bad moods or display negativity from time to time. Sometimes, it is best to simply ignore the occasional sour remark. Imagine the following scenario: Your family is gathered for dinner. As you begin serving the food, your eight-year-old suddenly bangs her cup on the table and yells, "Peas? I hate peas! Why do you have to make stupid peas?" Now, you can allow this statement to incite a heated argument by responding, "Do not call those peas 'stupid.' I worked hard to make a nice meal! I will not cater to your whims. Now apologize." Alternatively, you can save your energies for more important child-rearing battles. Look at her calmly and answer, "You don't like peas. That is okay; do not eat them." Then resume your meal.

Whenever possible, identify the root of your child's behavior. Defiant sassing or verbal outbursts may be caused by many things, including displaced anger, frustration, lack of appropriate communication skills, or a struggle for power or autonomy.

If you can identify the cause of the outburst, you can help your child find better ways of expressing herself. For example, perhaps you suspect your daughter's outburst was not really about peas but was because she felt jealous or ignored. Her cousin Jamie is over for dinner and loves peas. You could say, "I wonder if you think I am giving Jamie preferential treatment because I prepared his favorite vegetable. Tomorrow, I will make one of your favorites."

Verbal Battles

When you respond to your child's negativity or defiance, you are likely to wind up in a verbal battle. In addition, when your child was younger, he was often satisfied with simple cut-and-dried answers. Your older child now has the ability to see multiple perspectives to just about any issue. He is now aware of exceptions and nuances to every situation. Moreover, he now has a desire to discuss and argue these nuances.

Take—and Keep—Control

Two sides are needed for an argument. You have the power to choose to participate. Do you allow your child to push your buttons and cause you to respond in anger? When both you and your child are upset, it may be worthwhile to step back from the conflict. Declare a "cease-fire" until you both are calm. Then you may be able to share viewpoints and concerns. You may also wish to discuss how the battle began and got out of hand, so you can prevent future conflicts.

 **Fact**

For older children, conflict and arguments are usually over minor issues. Common topics of conflict include chores, schoolwork, money, dress styles, curfew, and friends. You may find battles over these same issues recurring.

Verbal battles can easily escalate. Even the most innocent comment may be misunderstood and hurtful to the other party. This table shows some sample statements that can escalate or calm an argument.

Argument Responses	
Calming statements	**Escalating statements**
What do you think?	You are too young to understand.
What else would you like to tell me?	I do not care.
I am listening.	You should not feel this way.
That sounds important to you.	I do not believe you.

Keep the Peace

You also have the power to divert the argument into a worthwhile discussion. Recognize that there are always two perspectives. Beyond the issue at hand, your child may be angry because she feels she is not being heard or respected. You may feel your child is not recognizing your authority. Ensure that each party has the opportunity to openly state her side without interruption. Show that you are listening to your child by using reflective listening, rephrasing what she is saying, and showing recognition of her message: "I hear that you are angry about your curfew."

You may wish to try the well-known technique of role-playing. This can be a good exercise to help each of you see the issue from the other's point of view. The rules are simple. Each person speaks as if she were the other. For example, you could say, "But Mom, I really don't think that it's fair for my bedtime to be so early." Then your daughter could say, "You know that I feel that you need to be in bed early on a school night." Focus the discussion on problem solving. Can you work together to generate a solution? For example, "What do you think we should try that would make us both feel better?"

There are also some fun ways to keep an argument under control. If these ideas sound silly, that is because they are! Sometimes a little humor is what you need to break the tension. Construct a pretend microphone. Only the person in possession of the microphone can speak. Another way to ensure each person has a turn airing his or her grievances without being interrupted is for the listener to wear a headpiece with large ears attached to it. To keep the give-and-take of sharing feelings fair, use a kitchen timer. Two minutes per turn is usually enough. Finally, if you really want to add some humor, insist that each person sing or pantomime their side of the argument.

When you reach a solution or come to an agreement, be sure to bring the conversation to a peaceful close. It is often helpful to restate the conclusion: "So, we agree that you can go to the zoo with your friends if you finish your homework first." You may even wish to seal the deal with a handshake or a hug.

Building Rapport

You may be able to prevent many temper tantrums and conflicts with your older child if you can maintain an overall positive relationship with him. For busy parents, it might seem difficult to find time for small talk, but it is often through a seemingly insignificant conversation that you can build rapport with your child. The comfortable back-and-forth of an everyday chat is a pleasure that reinforces your social and family connections. Importantly, these small conversations—about her favorite music or the current fashion colors or what modifications he's doing to his bicycle—mean that your child is much more likely to come to you when he or she has a big issue to discuss. If your only interactions with your child are to correct and argue, she will be much less likely to see you as a possible ally. Be accessible to and emotionally available for your child.

CHAPTER 15

Temper Tantrums in Public

W hen your child acts out in public, you suddenly feel like the victim of every parent's nightmare. It's hard to divert attention away from a screaming, yelling, or thrashing child. At times like these, you wish you could crawl into a hole and disappear. It seems like everyone is looking at you, and what you'd like to do is run away and hide, but after all, it's your child and you have to help him calm down. But how? What's the best way to handle this situation and prevent it from happening again? Curbing temper tantrums in public isn't easy, especially since there's extra pressure from an audience you never intended to have. The key is getting down to the right approach for your child, and believe it or not, it can be done.

Why Are Tantrums More Frequent in Public?

In truth, as a generalization, temper tantrums do not usually happen any more frequently in public than they do at home. Public tantrums may seem to occur more frequently because they are viewed as more troublesome or memorable. You may not easily recall the fit your child had over his spilled orange juice a few months ago, but the time he threw himself down on the ground screaming at Disneyland is an event no one will forget.

Some children do tend to have more temper tantrums in public. Even the most serene and even-tempered child may find the stimulation and excitement of some public locales overwhelming. Carnivals, festivals,

and even your local supermarket are places with loud noise, bright colors, and plenty of temptations. These factors can lead to a child's feeling stressed or agitated. In addition, other places come with too many adult demands for waiting and being quiet.

Alert!

Your adult brain is able to filter out much of the environmental stimuli around you. For example, you can tune out the sound of a barking dog, a fan, and a conversation in the next room to focus on a television show. This is not so easy for your young child. Places where she is bombarded with sensory input (loud noises, bright colors, flashing lights, etc.) are more likely to make her feel overwhelmed, agitated, or stressed out.

Coping with Your Anger and Embarrassment

When your child is on the verge of throwing a tantrum, whether it is at the park, in a restaurant, or in a store, your first reaction might be anger. After all, how many times have you tried to talk to your child about why this sort of behavior is inappropriate? You have probably tried to communicate your lack of tolerance for these sort of outbursts, and it might not have been at the best moment—midtantrum, for example. Yelling and getting frustrated won't help the situation, either. The angrier you get, the more upset your child will get. How, then, should you go about keeping your temper in check without giving in to your child?

It is normal to be concerned about how onlookers are viewing you. You worry your parenting skills are being judged. If you ignore your child, will they think you are being neglectful? If you reprimand your child, will they think you are too harsh? If you give in, will they think you are spoiling your child? It may be helpful to realize that at least some of the witnesses have gone through the same thing. These onlookers may empathize with you. In fact, most witnesses are more likely to feel sympathy for you rather than scorn.

Although it may be easier said than done, do not worry about what other people think. Just take a deep breath, stay calm, and focus on responding to your child. Pretend that you and your child are alone. Sometimes an onlooker may intervene, either by saying something or by trying to help. Whether they are supportive or critical, it is best to briefly smile at them and then return your focus to your child.

Maintaining Consistency

Recognize that your child can learn to have more temper tantrums in public if you respond to a public temper tantrum differently than you do to one at home. If, to avoid embarrassment or conflict in public, you give in to your child's demands, she will quickly learn that her tantrums are more effective and worthwhile in public. It may be tempting to give in to your child's demands, to avoid the temper tantrum that is bound to follow. Stand your ground and make it clear that her tantrum is not going to get her what she wants.

**Fact**

Studies show that, regardless of how a parent may respond to a temper tantrum at home, he or she often responds to public temper tantrums in one of two ways. Anger and embarrassment tend to cause parents to either harshly discipline their child or to give in to the child's demands.

Consistency is key. Respond to the temper tantrum in public in the same way that you would at home. If you ignore her at home, do the same at the store, even if this means pretending to read a cereal box. You may need to move your child to a quiet place, but in the long run, your child will learn there are set expectations for her behavior no matter where she is.

Prevention

Prevention is your first line of defense. You can prevent many problems simply by preparing in advance. Before you step out the door with your child, consider these ways to prevent many temper tantrums before they occur:

- **Be sure your child is well rested.** A tired child is more likely to become cranky. Most young children seem to fare better in the morning because they are more alert and not missing a needed naptime.
- **Never go hungry.** A hungry child is more likely to lose emotional calm and balance, especially in stressful or tiring situations.
- **Dress your child appropriately.** Comfortable clothes and shoes are important. Prepare for those hot stores by dressing your child in easy-to-remove layers. If your child is physically uncomfortable, it is likely that she will be cranky and more prone to having a tantrum.
- **Make a list.** When you have a child who is easily tempted and insists on having everything in the store he sees, try making a shopping list before the trip. Obtain a store flyer and encourage your child to choose one or two items in advance to be added to the list. Be sure to stick to this list in the store!
- **Review rules in advance.** Take time to review with the child what will be happening and how you will expect her to behave.
- **Choose child-friendly stores.** Some stores have removed "high temptation" items like candy and toys from the checkout area, or they have a candy-free checkout aisle. Other stores have child-sized shopping carts, which help your child feel that she is participating and being a "big" helper, which ultimately prevents her from growing bored, tired, or cranky. While it may not be the magic charm every time, it is helpful in occupying her mind.

 **Essential**

Plan to take your child on errands during off-peak times whenever possible. Grocery stores are often the most chaotic in the early evening and on weekends. Tuesday mornings are ideal. On the other hand, doctor offices seem to be the quietest early in the morning and on Friday afternoons.

General Strategies for Public Temper Tantrums

Not all outings will be a walk in the park or a day at the beach. Take heart, there are specific steps you can take to reduce and manage public meltdowns. The most important thing to remember, as mentioned above, is to stay calm. If you begin to raise your voice or become emotional, chances are your child's behavior will only escalate.

Prevent a Public Temper Tantrum

Engage your child. Even when the errand is not of interest to him, you can interact with him and keep his interest. Simply ask questions such as, "Who do you think could wear such teeny shoes?" or "How many people can you count in our line?"

Involve him. A child who is involved with the activity is less likely to become bored, restless, or frustrated. You might let him hold the coupon book or sort the items by color. Older children can help bag groceries and may even be able to contribute ideas for the day's agenda.

Have an emergency kit. Bring a little backpack or tote with age-appropriate items for times when your child has to wait or may be restless or cranky. Depending on your child's interests, it may include sticker books, picture books, handheld games, and more. Keep this in your car so it is readily available. Be sure to rotate items to maintain interest.

When Trouble Is Brewing

Respond promptly. It may be easy to react with "just wait until we get home," but this does very little to help a child regain calm and composure. In addition, by the time you get home and address the issue, it is unlikely the child will be able to associate the original behavior with the delayed consequences.

Be flexible. Be in tune with your child's moods and adjust your plans as needed. If you notice your child becoming fidgety in the shoe store, take a brief walk around the mall or stop for a pretzel before venturing on to the next store. Other early signs of trouble include increased crankiness and whining.

 **Fact**

Many malls and larger stores now have supervised play or activity areas set up. Such a place may be very welcome for your bored or restless child and a needed break for you.

Offer a snack. Even a small snack boosts blood sugar levels, energy, and mood. Keep a hidden stash of breadsticks or granola bars in your purse or glove compartment for a quick snack anytime.

Make concessions. Not everything has to be an all-or-nothing battle. Sometimes offering a limited choice breaks the cycle of power struggles. For example, "Although I can't let you have every toy you see, you may choose one doll if you walk through the rest of the store nicely with me."

Avoid leaving. Use the above strategies to help your child regain control. Do not simply give up on the errand or leave the location unless necessary. If you leave a location as soon as your child has a tantrum, she will quickly learn to manipulate you to avoid going to unpleasant places such as the doctor's office.

Find a refuge. When your child is having a full-fledged temper tantrum, take her to a quiet area away from the center of activity and traffic until you can help her calm down and regain control.

Strategies for Specific Places

Beyond the general guidelines, there are specific ways you can cope with your child's temper tantrums in a variety of settings. Each location or situation comes with its own set of potential challenges or problems that you may need to respond to.

Maybe We Should Order Takeout

Restaurants are a common setting for temper tantrums. You are probably asking your child to meet higher behavioral expectations than you would in the more informal home setting. Home may have a different set of rules. At home, you may allow her to leave the table when finished, or to get up and serve herself. In a restaurant, you ask your child to sit still, wait quietly, and exhibit his best manners, all while being hungry. You can cut down on the waiting time for your hungry child. Ask your waitress to bring rolls or an appetizer once you are seated. Buffets are ideal, and they have the added benefit of giving your child the chance to walk around a bit (with your supervision) and reduce her fidgetiness. When your child does have a temper tantrum, you will probably need to leave the table. Retreat to the restroom or lobby with your child.

 Essential

Look for restaurants that are child friendly. Many restaurants now do several things to accommodate families with young children. Some restaurants provide puzzle place mats, tablecloths that can be colored, or even tabletop toys.

If your child always seems hungry and impatient when you are waiting at a restaurant, pack a little snack that your child can munch on while she waits.

Just Sit and Wait

Doctor's offices and waiting rooms can be difficult places for a young child to remain calm and in control. Here again, you are asking your child to sit still and be quiet. Waiting rooms are notoriously uncomfortable places to be—the chairs are hard, the lights are harsh, and other people waiting may be uncomfortable or distraught. Unless you are in a pediatrician's office, it is unlikely there will be any toys, books, or pleasant distractions for your child. To make matters worse, your child may be ill or feeling anxious about the impending appointment. If your child has a meltdown, you may want to approach the receptionist. She may be able to delay your appointment until your child is calm. Conversely, if your child's temper tantrum is because of impatience, she may be able to arrange for you to be waited on sooner. It does not hurt to ask. Be sure to let her know if you are going to remove the child. Sometimes a trip to the water fountain or a brief stroll around the building will provide the distraction she needs.

To Market, to Market

A trip to the store can be challenging for a child. Shopping is simply not a fun activity for a young child. For what is usually an extended period, you are asking your child to either walk nicely by your side or to remain in a cart. They may see many attractive items that they find tempting but are not allowed to touch or have them. Remember that stores are often hot, crowded, and noisy, adding to a child's irritability and yours as well.

One mother shares, "My daughter was a reasonably calm and well-behaved child. This all changed when I would take her shopping for school clothes. I knew I could expect that, sometime during the day, she would become agitated and whiny and eventually have a full screaming tantrum in the middle of the dressing room. I was perplexed that she had no problems at grocery or hardware stores. Finally, it occurred to me to ask her if she knew why the department store made her feel so out of control. It turns out that she was getting static shocks from the clothing racks as she brushed by them, and then she was stepping on pins left on the dressing room floor! We started to shop at another store and she was fine."

Question?

What do I do once we are alone?
When your child is having a temper tantrum in public, find a refuge—a quiet area away from the center of activity and traffic. If you determine your child is having an attention-seeking tantrum, calmly tell him you will wait for him to stop before returning to the activity. If your child is having a tantrum for a developmental reason (frustration, poor verbal skills), patiently comfort him and address the issue at hand.

When Fun Places Are Not Fun

If your child has a temper tantrum at a fair, amusement park, or carnival, one of your first concerns needs to be safety. When your young child has a meltdown in one of these places, there is a risk that your child will run from you and be lost in the crowd or injured. If your child is losing control, your first step is to contain her. Get her to sit down on a bench or lead her over to a pavilion. If you determine that overexcitement and overstimulation are playing a part, find a place or activity for calming down. Many amusement parks offer more sedate activities that can be restful for both of you. Take a break from the wild rides and loud music and explore the surrounding gardens or the paddleboats on the lake. It is helpful to note, when your child has a temper tantrum in a "fun" place, leaving will not reinforce her tantrum and it may be an effective way to prevent further problems.

Going to Visit

Before visiting other people's homes, be sure to define the rules clearly to your child. Inform him of any special restrictions in advance. Can he pet the dog? Are there off-limits items in the host's house? If your child has a temper tantrum, calmly excuse yourself and your child to the bathroom or porch and help your child regain control. If your child is unable to calm down, you may need to end the visit.

Enjoying the Fine Arts

If your child has a tantrum in a movie theater, everyone around you will know. More than likely, your child's tantrum will be a disruption to the other theatergoers. Recognize that your child may be more likely to act up if the movie content is scary or too mature for her. Immediately take your child to a quiet space such as the bathroom or the lobby to regain control. Allow your child time to settle down completely. Be sure she is ready to go back into the theater. If you suspect that the problem will continue, it may be best to leave. Young children often enjoy live theater more than movies. Many cities have a children's theater program geared toward young children. These productions are usually lively and interactive, which helps engage children and make them less likely to become upset.

Going for a Ride

Maybe the worst place for a temper tantrum is on mass transit. You and your child are taking an eight-hour bus ride or flight to visit Grandma. Your child's toy rolls under the seat and it is not retrievable. Predictably, your child goes into hysterics. There are very few places to take your child aside. Whether you are taking the crosstown bus or a transatlantic flight, be sure to bring some activities or books. It may help if you can get a seat by the window. If your child has a tantrum, you may need to find refuge in the bathroom or in the back row of seats. If you are truly stuck, you can try holding him or rubbing his back. One mother faced with this situation came up with a creative idea. She draped a travel blanket over them both. This gave them some privacy. It also helped her out-of-control toddler to focus on her efforts to calm him down.

Public tantrums can, indeed, be particularly troublesome. However, as with tantrums at home, your calm and consistent response will result in diminishing displays of public temper tantrums.

CHAPTER 16

Temper Tantrums with Other Caregivers

Y ou have devoted a lot of effort to curbing your child's temper tantrums at home. You feel that you have made great strides in helping your child develop self-control and manage strong emotions such as anger and frustration. The problem is, the calm that you established exists only when your child is with you. When your child is with Grandma or at child care, she is still having many temper tantrums. How can you work with other caregivers and help them cope with your child's temper tantrums when you are not present?

Your Child's Behavior with Others

Your child may actually have more temper tantrums when he is with you than when he is with others. This is actually quite common and you should not take it personally. First, remember that you have probably directly taught your child to behave a certain way with other adults. Their behavior around other caregivers may be controlled and constricted. When your child is with you, he is comfortable and free to fully be himself. Your child trusts you and knows it is safe to "let it all hang out." He can feel secure in knowing that you will accept him, love him, and keep him safe, even if he loses control.

A good example of this can be seen with three-year-old Katie. It was clear to Katie's preschool teacher that Katie was unhappy being away from Mom and that she was reluctant to participate in preschool activities.

However, Katie did not cry or whine for her mother. Rather, she was sullen, quiet, and somewhat withdrawn. When Katie's mother came to pick her up, Katie fell to pieces. She was crying so hard that her mother mistakenly thought that Katie was not glad to see her. To the contrary, now Katie felt safe to let go of the strong emotions that she was holding in all day.

Your child is bound to behave differently for other people. This is human nature. We all act differently depending on where we are or whom we are interacting with. You behave very differently when you are at work, interacting with a client, than you do when you are at home alone with your spouse. The same will be true for your child. In fact, you probably encourage it. It is likely that you have encouraged your child, from a very early age, to behave differently in public than he does at home. You may urge your child to use "their special manners" when Aunt Carol comes for a visit.

Behave Yourself

Generally, most parents take active steps to help their child learn to interact with others appropriately. Oftentimes, these standards of behavior are more stringent than they are for behavior at home. You may teach your child very specific manners or codes of conduct. For example, "Address other adults by their last name" or "When we visit Grammy, we have to remember to sit only on the plastic-covered couch."

 **Essential**

You will probably not be able to predict how your child will behave when you leave her in the care of another adult. Even if your child appears to listen and respect that person in your presence, your child's behavior may be very different once you have gone.

Tantrums with Others

However, your child may be more likely to exhibit misbehavior or have temper tantrums while in the care of another adult. This may be true for all other adults or just a select few. Surely, the unique and personal interaction that these adults and your child share will affect your child's behavior. However, these are a few general reasons why your child my have more temper tantrums while she is in the care of another adult.

Stress

Stress may be a strong reason for your child's temper tantrums. This may be particularly true if your child does not know the caregiver well. The child may also feel additional stress if the caregiving is to happen in an unfamiliar place. You may be able to avoid some problems by simply requesting that the adult care for your child in your home rather than in their home.

Separation and Favoritism

Whether your child knows the caregiver well or not, do not discount the possibility of separation anxiety. Some children may even have difficulty being left alone with a close family member. One mother shares, "We have a close-knit, happy family. My two-year-old son is generally a happy, calm, and easygoing child. By all appearances, he adores his father. Dad and he get along famously, like little buddies, when we are all at home together. The problem is when I need to leave him with Dad. Then, all of a sudden, only Mom will do! You would think that I am trying to leave him with an ogre . . . if you could see how he carries on. My husband is unable to console or calm his son and it breaks my husband's heart."

Testing Limits

While you have been raising and disciplining your child, you have been setting down clear expectations and parameters for their behavior. Children need the sense of security of knowing that someone will limit their behavior and keep them safe. Children also need to learn by direct experience what those limits are and what the consequences are for exceeding those limits. You may or may not have gone through a stage with your child where she is actively testing the limits. Regardless, your child may be compelled to reenter the process with every new caregiver. She may be thinking things like, "Okay, I know that I must pick up my toys at home, but what about at day care?" "Daddy won't let me watch cartoons, but maybe the babysitter will." "Mom ignores me when I scream for a cookie, but I wonder if Grandma will give in."

Essential

You can minimize the potential for your child to have temper tantrums with other caregivers by limiting the number of people who care for your child. The more stability there is for your child, the less stress and uncertainty he faces. Children will have more emotional maturity and control when they can form close attachments with a select few consistent caregivers.

There will be unavoidable times when you will need to have someone care for your child. Whether this is a onetime event of a few hours or a full-time arrangement, your child may have increased difficulty maintaining emotional control, and therefore, she will be more prone to temper tantrums. Whenever possible, prepare your child in advance. Let her know what will be happening and what she can expect. Be very clear and specific about how you expect her to behave in these situations. Avoid vague directives like "be nice at child care" or "don't misbehave for Aunt Nancy." Tell your child in a positive way exactly what you expect her to do: "When you are at child care, I want you to use your words if you are angry with other children." "Follow your aunt Nancy's rules and pet her dog gently."

Tantrums with a Relative

It is likely that there will be a time when a family member will care for your child. This may occur on an as-needed basis or perhaps he or she will be caring for your child every day. There are both pros and cons to having a relative provide child care for your child.

You do need to consider if this person is the best person to care for your child. Here are some questions to ask:

- Is this person patient with children?
- Is she physically able to chase or carry a young child, if needed?
- Will she supervise your young child at all times?
- Does she have some experience with or knowledge of child development and guidance?
- Can she keep your child safe and healthy? (CPR and first-aid training are desirable.)

Relative Care on a Regular Basis

There are many reasons why relative child care may be the best option for your family. Relative care may be the most convenient and accessible option, especially if the caregiver will be someone who lives in the child's home or nearby. Relative child care may be the option that you feel the most comfortable with. Perhaps the only person you will trust with the care of your child is your own mother. You can be assured that your child will receive more individualized attention than he would at a child care center. Finally, you may have more flexibility with both cost and scheduling when making child care arrangements with a family member.

Specific Issues

When a relative is caring for your child, there may be specific issues that arise that can lead to your child's having a temper tantrum. Most problems will occur because there is a lack of consistency between your child-rearing philosophy and approach and that of the relative caregiver. Almost any difference between the way you and the relative interact with your child can open the door for her to test limits. An older child in particular will look for exceptions and caveats to the rules that she may have at home. By establishing consistent discipline policies that match what you do at home, you can avoid the famous whine, "But Grandma lets me . . . "

 **Fact**

Relative child care is still very popular. At one time or another, upward of 45 percent of all parents will call on a family member to care for their child. In rural areas where child care programs are scarce, as many as 75 percent of parents will choose a relative for child care.

A relative caregiver may wish to ensure that the child has fun and enjoys his company. Therefore, he may feel guilty or reluctant to enforce the rules and limits that you have set. Reassure him that there are ways that he can "spoil" or "treat" your child without allowing the child to break or bend the guidelines you have set for appropriate behavior.

How to Maintain Consistency

There is one best way to prevent and manage your child's temper tantrums when they're with another caregiver: consistency. Your child needs to know that your expectations for her behavior do not change. Temper tantrums will be responded to in the same fashion, all of the time. For example, you decided that you will ignore your child when she has a temper tantrum because she wants a cookie before dinner. This means that you will ignore her if this happens at the store and that you will ignore her if this happens at the neighbor's annual barbecue picnic. This also means that your neighbors will ignore the tantrum and so will Grandpa and Uncle Bobby. Once there is a broken link in the chain, there will be a problem. If Uncle Bobby gives in to your child's tantrum just once, you can surely expect that your child's temper tantrum behavior will increase when she visits Uncle Bobby.

Before a relative cares for your child, even if only for a few hours, it is wise to communicate clearly to her how you manage and guide your child's behavior and temper tantrums.

Challenges with Grandparents

The most common and popular relative child care arrangement is with your child's grandparents. Along with the special joy that may come with intergenerational care, there are unique challenges regarding establishing discipline policies for your own child.

Most grandparents will have an opinion on how you should raise your children and manage their behavior. They will usually feel like they have some competence and expertise on the matter; after all, look how good you turned out! Remember, grandparents' concerns and opinions are usually a sign that they feel love and commitment to you and your child.

It is normal that you may feel uncomfortable sharing parenting strategies with in-laws or your own parents. If you are using a different approach than they did, you may worry that you are offending or hurting them. It is possible that you will feel judged or scrutinized for your own parenting abilities as well. It may be helpful to remind yourself that, in this situation, you are both an adult and the parent.

Essential

In spite of your best efforts, you may find that the grandparents are overly judgmental or critical about the way that you are managing your child's behavior. If it is clear that you cannot establish a consistent approach for your child or you doubt that they will honor your wishes, then you should consider finding a new caregiver for your child.

Tips to Reach Agreement

There are specific ways that you can communicate with grandparents as you try to establish a consistent approach to your child's behavior. Use humor when you can. Perhaps find common ground by asking Grandma to share some stories of your worst temper tantrums.

Nowadays, when parents look for child-rearing advice, they turn to doctors, books, or the Internet. Do not forget that grandparents have a wealth of experience and will want to feel valued. When possible, involve them in decision making. Do not be afraid to ask them for advice, but remember that you are not obligated to take it.

Set up a specific plan for managing your child's behavior in advance. Be sure to review strategies that you use at home for preventing temper tantrums, such as avoiding fatigue, hunger, and over-stimulating places.

Here is just a partial list of possible situations you may wish to plan for. Decide together how grandparents should respond to the child when:

- She cries when you leave
- He grabs a toy from another child
- She has a meltdown because a toy is too difficult for her
- He gets angry and bites his cousin
- She has a temper tantrum when it is time for a nap
- He screams and kicks when Grandpa will not buy him a toy at the store
- She gets frustrated when trying to put on her shoes

Describe in detail how you want the grandparents to respond to your child's temper tantrums. Be specific and try to cover all of the possible scenarios. At home, you may respond very differently to a temper tantrum that is caused by fear than a temper tantrum that is staged to get your attention.

Alert!

Although you ideally want consistency between you and the caregiver, when managing your child's behavior, not everything has to be the same. Grandparents do not have to follow every rule you have to a T. It is okay if they allow your child some special privileges or choose to impose their own house rules as well.

Tantrums in Child Care

Anyone who cares for your child for any length of time will have an impact on his development and behavior. Therefore, you will want to use great care in selecting a child care provider. Ideally, you want to find someone who will work together with you to guide and teach your child.

There are many child care options to consider. Each one has its drawbacks and its benefits. Only you can choose what is the best option for both you and your child. Here are the most popular three child care options.

Nannies

A nanny may live in or out of your home. With a nanny, you will have the most influence and control over your child's care. You will be able to dictate all policies and rules as you choose. A nanny will be exclusively devoted to the care of only your child. Keep in mind that a nanny may not have the same level of education and training as family or center care providers, and nannies are usually the most expensive child care option.

Family Day Care Providers

A family day care provider takes children into her own home, usually while she is caring for her own children. She may be either registered or licensed by the state. The group size will be a lot smaller than a center program but will often be a mixed age group. Infants through school age will be all together. Consequently, your young toddler could be with a group of four- and five-year-olds, or your school-ager may be spending his day with infants and toddlers. A family day care provider may be somewhat flexible regarding your requests, but it is wise to be sure that you agree on basic child guidance and discipline approaches before enrolling your child.

 *Question?*

How can I find a high-quality program?
You want to make sure that the program is licensed or registered. This tells you that the program meets minimum standards of health and safety. Programs that received accreditation have met even higher standards of quality.

Center Programs

If you want your child to have experience interacting and playing with children her own age, then a child care center may be the best bet for you. Because child care centers are the most regulated, staff and teachers are most likely to have the highest level of training and education in child development and behavior. Child care centers are also the most likely to provide your child with enrichment and school readiness activities. On the other hand, large group size means less individualized attention for your child. Recognize that you will have considerably less influence over the program's policies, so it will be up to you to find a program that suits you and your child.

Before Starting Child Care

Before enrolling your child with a child care provider or hiring a nanny, sit down and discuss your values and beliefs about child rearing and guidance with them. Also, take the time to listen to his or her approach to managing children's behavior. You will find as many different approaches as there are providers. You want someone who basically agrees with your approach and, more importantly, is willing to work with you as a partner to provide consistent care for your child.

Get to Know the Provider

Ask the provider how she manages children's behavior, how she uses discipline, and how she responds to temper tantrums. Because they are usually caring for groups of children rather than one child, family day care providers and center providers will typically respond to temper tantrums in a slightly different way than you do at home.

Because the child care provider has a background in child development as well as managing groups of children, a majority of her behavioral management techniques will be focused on prevention. Room arrangement, daily scheduling, and seating plans are things that she will consider as she strives to prevent misbehavior and temper tantrums from the children in her care.

She may ignore minor upsets and temper tantrums, often encouraging older children to resolve conflicts with only some minor guidance or intervention. When things get out of hand and children become aggressive, she may use time-out more than you would at home. This may simply be because it is the most effective way for her to keep all of the children safe and in control.

Share about Your Child

In order to make sure that you and the child care provider agree on how to manage your child's temper tantrums, take the time to share your views and information about your child. It will be beneficial if you share with the provider specific information about your child's temper tantrums. Here are possible things to mention:

- Known triggers
- Problematic times of the day
- The impact of hunger or fatigue on your child's behavior
- How your child manages strong emotions such as anger and frustration
- Your child's verbal skills
- What calms your child
- How you respond to temper tantrums at home

Challenges in Child Care

Once your child is in a child care setting, you may witness temper tantrums as a result of new issues or triggers that are associated with the child care experience. Remember, you are asking your child to adapt to a new environment, new people, and a new schedule all at once. If your child is slow to adapt, you are bound to witness your child having difficulty early on.

Also remember, your child will be facing a new set of expectations, limits, and guidelines. It may be difficult for your child to learn the following: in child care, I am allowed to____, but at home, I cannot ____. Your child may also feel some stress as she tries to get used to a more structured daily schedule. Additionally, a brightly colored, ornately decorated, busy, and noisy classroom may be overstimulating for your child.

Fact

Child care turnover affects young children. Young children will become attached to their caregivers in much the same way that they do with their parents. The departure of a caregiver can be very upsetting and stressful. Studies show that when infants and toddlers go through many providers, they tend to perform less well in preschool.

One of the biggest benefits to enrolling your child in a child care center is that she will have opportunities to interact with other children her own age. This will help promote her language skills as well as important social skills, including cooperation, negotiation, conflict resolution, and sharing. If your child is prone to temper tantrums because she is egocentric or she has difficulty sharing, interacting with other children in a group setting may be particularly helpful in eventually helping your child build skills to overcome those problems. This will not happen overnight, though. Be aware that if your child has not had much exposure to other children her own age, you may initially see an increase in her temper tantrums as she begins to learn to adapt her behavior to meet the expectations for group interactions and dynamics.

Separation Anxiety in Child Care

Possibly the most common cause of temper tantrums with a child care provider will be separation anxiety. Separation anxiety and tantrums will be most prevalent for children ages ten months to three years of age, children who have never been away from you, and children who are not securely attached to you. You can read more about the causes for separation anxiety in Chapter 6.

Make a Plan
Work together with your child care provider. She deals with this

issue on almost a daily basis, and together you should be able to devise a strategy that will make good-byes an easier time for all of you. Do not wait for the first separation temper tantrum. There are things you can do to prevent problems. Prepare your child in advance; tell him what will be happening and what he can expect. Make the transition gradual. Arrange to visit the program with your child at least once; let him tour the room and meet the teacher. Whenever possible, spend a little time in the program with your child for the first few days. Avoid just rushing out the door.

 *Essential*

There are some wonderful children's books that you can choose to read to your child to help prepare her. Here are some good ones to start with: *Adam's Daycare* by Julie Ovenell-Carter, *Carl Goes to Daycare* by Alexandra Day, and *Going to Daycare* by Fred Rogers.

Time to Say Good-bye

You may find it helpful if you establish a good-bye routine and then stick with it. Perhaps you will always help her hang up her jacket, give her a hug, and once inside the classroom, wave at her through the door. Avoid lingering or going back for "just one more hug." In the long run, this makes good-byes even more difficult.

Although this separation may be difficult for you as well, stay positive. Avoid dramatizing the event with statements like, "Oh, sweetie, I am so, so sorry I have to leave you here!" Instead, paint the picture in a positive way by saying something like, "While I am at work today, you will be able to stay in the fun school and play with other children." Do not forget to reassure your child that he can always count on the fact that you will be returning for him. It may be helpful if you can give him a concrete idea of when to expect you: "I will pick you up right after snacktime."

CHAPTER 17

Preventing Temper Tantrums

Temper tantrums are a normal part of your young child's behavior. It is unrealistic to expect that you will be able to prevent them all. You can, however, recognize some of the common triggers and causes of many of your child's temper tantrums. Once you can identify potential causes, you can prevent many tantrums before they happen.

How Limits Prevent Tantrums

The more self-control your child has, the less likely she will be to have temper tantrums. Self-control allows your child to regulate and control her emotions. Learning self-control is an ongoing process that occurs with your support and discipline. Your child needs limits and external boundaries in order for her to internalize rules and standards of behavior that will allow her to develop self-control.

The Need for Limits

Your child has a deep-rooted need for limits on his behavior. The limits and boundaries that you set for your child's behavior will make him feel secure. Some children will directly ask for guidance or limits if they feel they need them. This is particularly true when a child is in a new situation where there may be less structure and fewer rules. A child who is raised with a lot of structure and rules may enter a more lax environment and start to ask, "Is it okay if

I . . . ?" "Are we allowed to . . . ?" You may even witness your child putting himself in time-out when he gets upset. He may ask you what is allowed or acceptable in a given situation. He needs to know that an adult is there to guide him and keep him safe and in control. When he is feeling confused, scared, frustrated, angry, or overwhelmed, he will count on you to guide him with authority and control.

 Essential

Setting limits and boundaries on your child's behavior does not mean taking away her freedom or autonomy. You can still allow your child to have many choices within the parameters that you set. For example, "Playing ball in the street is not safe. You can play ball or another game that you choose, but you must stay in the yard."

No Rules?

If you choose to set very few or no limitations on your child's behavior, she will have a difficult time learning safe, appropriate behavior and self-control. You are handing over to your child the control to regulate her own behavior. This parenting style or approach is known as permissive parenting. Permissive parents will usually establish very few rules and often do not consistently enforce the rules that they have set. Due to a lack of your child's experience, and her cognitive and emotional immaturity, this approach is rarely effective and is bound to be a disaster. Can you imagine what would happen if you said to your toddler, "I have laid out your pajamas for you. I trust you to know when you are tired. You can decide when you are ready to go to bed." Or, "I see that your teeth are bothering you. Let me know if you wish to go to the dentist."

When your child fails at regulating her own behavior, she will be more likely to have outbursts and temper tantrums and to lose her self-control. She will not be making independent decisions. Eventually, she will rely on others to control her decisions and actions. If you do not set and enforce limits for her, school or even law authorities may need to do so later on in her life.

Setting Limits

By establishing rules, you are setting limits and parameters for your child's safe and acceptable behavior. These rules should become guidelines that clearly communicate your expectations. When you establish rules for your child, there are many things to consider.

Who Writes the Rules?

Obviously, when your child is very young, you will take sole responsibility for establishing all rules and codes of conduct. Once your child is past three years old, you should consider involving her when you are generating the rules. There are many benefits to involving your child. If she is involved in a discussion about potential rules, she will be more likely to understand their importance. She will be more likely to comply with rules she thought of and agreed with. Additionally, she will be less likely to view rules as arbitrary or unfair.

If contributing to the household rules is a difficult task for your young child, try to make it more concrete and realistic. Take a piece of poster board and draw a line down the middle. Label one column "DO" and the other column "DON'T." Ask your child what he can do to be safe, for items to put in the "DO" column, and what is not safe or nice behavior, for the "DON'T" column. Try to draft your list of rules mainly from the "DO" list and state the rules in a positive way.

Three difficulties may arise when you try to involve your older child in generating a rule list.

- She may not wish to participate. If this is the case, just go ahead and create the list without her.
- She creates too many detailed rules. For example, "No bouncing tennis balls in the house. No kicking soccer balls

in the house. No rolling balls down the steps." If this happens, help her create a more general rule: "All ball playing stays outside."

- She creates rules that are unreasonable or impossible for everyone to adhere to. For example, "Everyone can have only four ounces of water to drink before bedtime. Only children older than five can watch TV. You must brush your teeth each and every time you eat chocolate or anything brown." If this occurs, ask your child to consider the fairness of the rule and if she will truly be able and willing to follow it herself.

Keep Your Expectations Clear

The rules should be a clear statement of your expectations for your child's behavior. Rules should be brief and to the point. Avoid rules that include exceptions and variable factors. Here is an example of such a rule: "Don't stay out past 8 P.M. on school nights unless you already have permission or you call before 7 P.M. to ask for this time to be extended. Both parents must agree that you may stay out later than 8 P.M., unless one parent cannot be reached before 7:30 P.M. If only one parent is contacted, you must return home by 8:30 P.M. to secure further permission." Not only is this rule confusing, but it leaves a lot of room for your child to attempt to negotiate for leniency.

Keep Your Expectations Specific

Do not expect your child to be a mind reader. State your expectations very specifically. Parents often just tell children directives such as "be nice," "be good for Grandma," and "don't act up!" Remember that your standards or ideals of what is "well behaved" will probably be vastly different from what your child considers "well behaved." When you tell your ten-year-old that you want his room to be clean, you are envisioning a room where all of the books are lined up in alphabetical order, the bed is made with fresh sheets, and his floor is mopped and waxed. Conversely, your ten-year-old believes a clean room to be a room where all of the dirty laundry is hidden under the bed. Other examples of vague rule statements include "calm down" and "help out."

State Rules Positively

Rules should state what behavior you expect. Tell your child what to do. Avoid negatively phrased rules. Younger children, in particular, will focus on the action and disregard the negation. For example, when you tell your preschooler, "Do not go near the swimming pool without an adult," he focuses on the phrase "go near the swimming pool." "Stop pulling the cat's tail" becomes "pull the cat's tail." You can change a rule from negative to positive just by changing a few words.

Changing Negative Rules	
Negative Rules	**Become Positive Rules**
No running in the house.	Walk while you are in the house.
You may not eat in the living room.	Food stays in the kitchen.
Candy before dinner is not allowed.	Candy is allowed only after dinner.
No watching TV before your homework is done.	Do your homework before you watch TV.

If you look at the negative rules above, you can see how ambiguous they can be, especially to a child who is testing limits. When you say, "No running in the house," your child may ask, "What about galloping, sprinting, or spinning?" When you say, "You may not eat in the living room," they may ask, "What about my bedroom?" Notice how the positive rules are clear and defined, leaving less room for questioning.

Alert!

Toddlers can be very literal and rigid when they hear and interpret rules. When you say, "Food stays in the kitchen," your toddler may insist that Spike's food bowls be brought up from the garage. Additionally, your young toddler may overgeneralize a rule. For example, when you allow him to use soap paint on the bathtub walls, he may think painting on any walls with any type of paint is okay.

Choosing Rules

Although you want your expectations to be clear, it is neither wise nor practical to list a rule for every possible infraction. First, you will never be able to anticipate all of your child's future misbehaviors. Second, you will end up with a list of rules more lengthy and complex than the federal tax code. Consider your priorities. Pick just a few clear and easy-to-remember rules that you feel will serve as guidelines in helping your child learn safe behavior and self-control. Consider your child's developmental abilities. Make sure the rules reflect reasonable expectations for her age and maturity. For example, requiring your three-year-old to make her bed independently each and every morning is a rule that will be difficult for her to comply with. If you want your child to remember and internalize your rules, keep the list short. For children under school age, three to five rules are optimal. Even for older children, keep the lists short; after all, there are only ten commandments.

Three Basic Rules

To keep expectations simple, you can set a few broad rules that can encompass your expectations of your child's behavior. Here are three suggested rules. You will find they are clear, easy to remember, and will cover just about any misbehavior you would want to respond to.

Be Safe to Others

"Others" can include friends, family member, pets, and so forth. Unsafe behaviors include hitting, biting, grabbing, and teasing or name-calling (which "hurts" feelings). You may wish to explain to your child that you will not allow anyone to hurt him and you will not allow him to hurt others. You will also refer to the rule if he is hurting you.

Be Safe to Yourself

You can remind your child that it is important to you that he stay safe and healthy. This rule includes all behaviors that are unsafe to the child (running with scissors, playing in the busy street) and can also include behaviors that protect his health (hand washing, eating nutritious foods).

Be Safe to Things

You are asking your child to respect all toys, materials, and property. Behaviors that fall under this rule include breaking toys and coloring on walls. You can refer to this rule the next time your toddler dumps all of your papers out of your briefcase!

Enforcing Rules and Limits

How you respond to misbehavior and how you enforce limits will send strong messages to your child. You are showing her what behavior you expect and value. You are showing her that she can depend on you to help her regain and maintain control when she is acting out or having a temper tantrum.

Rules in Priority

Focus your enforcement on the rules that are most important in helping your child learn safe behavior and self-control. It is okay to allow some minor infractions. For the sake of your own sanity, pick your battles and do not sweat the small stuff. Perhaps, you want your child to eat nutritious food at every meal. Dinnertime rolls around and you become locked in a battle with your child. You are planning to serve peas but she wants asparagus instead. In the grand scheme of things, will it really matter if she has asparagus instead of peas? In fact, if your ultimate motivation is her health, a few meals without a vegetable serving at all will do no harm. Do not let the original rules or intent get lost in a battle of wills.

Question?

What behaviors can I ignore?
Almost any misbehavior you will encounter will fall under the three basic rules. Behaviors that do no harm, directly or indirectly, are often best ignored. These behaviors include tattling, whining, pouting, and bathroom or silly talk. In fact, responding to these types of behaviors will usually increase their frequency.

State the Reason for the Rule

Always try to state the reason for a rule as you enforce it. Your explanation does not need to be a lengthy lecture; a brief statement will do. For example, "Put your feet on the floor. It is not safe for you to climb on the railing. You could fall." "Return the scissors to their case so no one gets stabbed by them." When you state the reason for a rule, your child will be less likely to see the rule as arbitrary or as just your way of exerting power. Explanation statements such as "Because I am the dad" or "Because I said so" are statements that will surely be met with resistance by your child and do not teach anything.

Most importantly, when you repeatedly state the reason for a rule, you are helping your child learn the consequences of his actions, and you are promoting the development of his inner voice or conscience.

See how this occurs in this example: Your five-year-old keeps jumping on your bed. Each time you catch her, you tell her, "Stop jumping on my bed." When she whines, "But why?" you snap, "Because I say stop. Now go outside to play and do not let me catch you jumping on the bed again." She obediently leaves, but only until she sees that you are in the laundry room and she does not think you will catch her. She continues to sneak into your room and jump on your bed. Then you read this book. The next time you see her jumping on the bed, you say, "I want you to stop jumping on my bed. It is not safe. You could bounce off and hit your head. If you want to jump safely, go outside." The next time she approaches your bed, there is a good chance she will stop and think, "Even if I will not be caught, it is a bad idea for me to jump on the bed. I do not want to hit my head." She has now begun to internalize the rule and develop self-control. Finally, it is important to note that, if you are unable to explain or justify a rule, you should reconsider whether it is a fair or reasonable rule.

 Essential

Empty threats are poisonous to both your child's behavior and your authority. It is wise and acceptable to tell your child the potential consequences of her actions: "If you throw those blocks one more time, I will put them away." However, it is critical that you follow through. If not, your child will quickly learn to disregard your threats in much the same way the village disregarded the boy who cried wolf.

Consistent Enforcement

As your child is learning what it is that you expect from him, he is also learning what to expect from you. Consistently respond and enforce the limits and rules that you have set. Lax enforcement of your rules is no better than not having any rules at all. For example, you have told your child that he may not play in the living room. The last few times you found him playing there, you removed the toys he was playing with and sent him to his room. However, on one occasion, you were in the middle of cooking dinner and it had been a hectic day for you. You decided to let this misbehavior slide, just once, promising yourself that you will be sure to punish him for both offenses the next time you see him. The problem is, your child may interpret this by thinking he can get away with the misbehavior whenever you are busy or harried. Additionally, with rare exception, a rule should apply no matter where the child is, what time of day it is, or who is enforcing the rule. If not, your child will quickly learn that rules she can bend are the easiest rules to break.

And so, if Dad allows your child to stay up later than you do, there may be conflict. Your child may even learn to play one parent against the other. You will find that the most effective way to change and influence your child's behavior is to have all caregivers respond to and manage your child's behavior in a set and consistent fashion. In Chapter 16, you will find tips for working with other relatives and child care providers for this very objective.

Reducing Stress

It is easy to view childhood as a carefree time, a time of lots of freedom and few worries or responsibilities. The truth is, you cannot completely shelter your child from the up-and-down stresses of daily life. Even in the most idyllic childhood, there is disappointment and loss. As it is with adults, stress affects a child's demeanor and behavior. A child who is experiencing stress is far more likely to be irritable, oversensitive, and prone to temper tantrums. Although you cannot remove all stress from your child's life, you can buffer him from its effects. You can reduce many temper tantrums simply by recognizing that he is feeling stress, and responding to him with empathy.

Causes of Stress

Many things could be stressful for your child. Realize that each child is different, and some children are more resilient than others. For example, one child may react to the death of a pet goldfish by calmly requesting a trip to the pet store for a replacement. Another grieving child may be inconsolable, vowing to never love another animal for as long as she lives. There is a long list of events or experiences that may prove stressful for your child. A few of these include illness, divorce, moving, death of a family member, new school, a fight with a sibling, losing a favorite toy, or nightmares. In fact, just about any change in your child's life or routine may be stressful.

 **Fact**

Positive occurrences can also be stressful for your child. Many of these events are preceded by a lot of anticipation and excitement, which can be overwhelming for a young child. A few of the events include holiday celebrations, birthdays, vacation travel, and starting school.

Signs of Stress

Each child will exhibit stress in a different way. Observe your child carefully. Changes in her habits or routines are often a strong indicator that she is experiencing stress.

Here are some common signs of stress in young children:

- **Change in sleep habits.** Your child starts having difficulty falling asleep at night, or maybe she is beginning to wake up in the middle of the night. She may start grinding her teeth. Nightmares or night terrors may become more frequent.
- **Change in eating habits.** You may notice that your child suddenly becomes finicky at mealtimes. If he is stressed, his appetite could either decrease or increase.
- **Change in social interactions.** Your once popular child is having difficulties interacting with others. Perhaps she has become sullen or defiant. She may become more aggressive or have a hard time sustaining play activities.
- **Change in mood or personality.** Your once cheerful, independent child has become overly sensitive, demanding, or clingy.

- **Change in other habits.** Your child may exhibit other signs of stress, including stuttering, nail biting, hair twirling, regression, or self-stimulation.

One mother shares how she finally recognized that her three-year-old son was experiencing stress.

I thought I had it all under control. When I was preparing to have my second child, I spent a lot of time preparing Trevor for the arrival of the baby. I read books to him and involved him in picking out the baby furniture, the whole nine yards. He seemed as excited as everyone else waiting for the baby to be born. He seemed thrilled when I finally brought his little sister home from the hospital. He never said anything negative and he still maintained a cheery attitude like normal. Nevertheless, I did start to notice something odd. He was starting to act more and more like a baby himself. He started to insist that he also drink out of a bottle. Then, what really made me realize he was not as happy as he seemed, was when, after seven months without a problem, he started to pee his bed again!

Responding to a Stressed Child

The way you respond to your child gives you the ability to alleviate much of your child's stress. First, if you are able, eliminate or reduce the source of your child's stress. Be sure to respond to your child with compassion and empathy. Listen carefully to her concerns. Acknowledge her feelings with statements like, "I can see that you are upset because your friend is moving" or "I understand how much the upcoming math test is worrying you."

Know what is calming for your child. If touch is calming for him, try hugs, massages, or even a warm bath. If activity is calming for him, try some silly dancing or go for a long walk together. Recognize that what may be soothing for one child may be agitating for another. Rollicking rock music may help one child calm down and yet be too stimulating for another.

Prepare for Stress

Since change is a common stress for young children, whenever possible, prepare your child in advance. Imagine the shock you would feel if you arrived home one evening to find all your belongings packed in boxes. Your spouse announces, "Surprise! I've found a wonderful new house; we are moving tonight." We all need time to adjust to change. Take time to discuss the upcoming event with your child.

Essential

Reading a children's book about a similar topic can help your child prepare for a stressful event. He can identify with the characters and see what to expect. A positive conclusion to the story can be very reassuring.

Some events you may wish to prepare your child for could include starting school or hospitalization. Whenever possible, arrange for your child to visit such settings in advance. Many of these places now have tours and programs designed specifically for this very purpose. Once you mention the event to your child, she may have many concerns and questions. Your availability and willingness to respond openly will help to alleviate her stress. As your child matures, you can begin to teach her skills for coping with stress. Chapter 18 has a section on helping your child learn self-calming skills.

Adding Structure

You can prevent many temper tantrums by adding structure. By adding structure to your child's schedule and environment, you can reduce many triggers for temper tantrums, including frustration, struggles for autonomy, insecurity, and fatigue.

Take a look at your child's physical environment, particularly the places where he spends a lot of time, such as his bedroom or playroom. Look for ways to make this a safe place for him to be independent and able to explore. Whenever possible, arrange toys and materials so they are accessible. You can also reduce your child's frustration by removing breakable and unsafe objects. This will minimize the times you will have to say no to your child and restrict him. By promoting your child's independence, you also build his confidence and self-control.

A child needs to have a sense of calm and order in her life. You can accomplish this by structuring her day. She will feel more in control when there are daily routines that follow a predictable pattern. She will learn what to expect, and she can begin to anticipate how to deal with it. A day without any predictable routine is very chaotic and disturbing to a young child. For example, it is midmorning and your toddler is playing in the yard. She is happily chasing butterflies when you call to her, "Okay, stop now and come with me." She freezes and looks at you, seemingly puzzled. You continue, "Let's go. I want you to take a nap now." Your demand is sure to meet with some resistance. If, on the other hand, you have a set routine for naptime at the same time each day, she will come to internalize your expectations and be more likely to comply.

CHAPTER 18

Teaching Skills

Y ou are finding that your six-year-old daughter still has many temper tantrums and episodes when she loses control. She is very compliant and quick to calm down and respond to your guidance. You can easily help her solve problems and manage the crisis. The problem is, when you are not around, she cannot control her own behavior. You know you will not be able to hover over her every waking moment. What can you do?

Helping Your Child Develop Self-Control

Much of parenting is connecting with your child and guiding your child's behavior. You must intervene to stop or redirect your child when his behavior is inappropriate or unsafe, much as a police officer would. Children without self-control may behave appropriately in your presence but continue to act out or sneak things when you are not there. Of course, you cannot always be there; eventually your child needs to make independent choices and control her own behavior. This is the goal of self-control, to internalize rules and standards of behavior.

There are many skills for your child to master to learn self-control. In many cases, you can provide experiences of direct instruction to promote self-control. You do not have to wait for opportunities to occur naturally.

Reducing Impulsiveness

Becoming less impulsive is a big part of self-control. Children naturally react to situations impulsively. When distressed or angered, they
are inclined to lash out emotionally. An impulsive child acts first and
thinks later. In other words, she looks before she leaps.

The goal is for your child to pause and recognize how she feels
and wishes to act. Then she needs to evaluate the possible consequences of the behavioral choices she could make. She needs to fore-
see, "If I ____, then ___ will happen." For example, "If I leave my socks
on the porch, then they will get wet and muddy." At first, getting your
child to stop while she is preparing to act is tricky. It is best when you
can catch your child at this moment. For example, your child has
been arguing with a playmate and now you see him swinging a large
block near his friend's head. Stop your child when you see he is acting impulsively. Do this with physical contact or even a signal such
as a whistle or clearing your throat. Some parents are able to master
"the look." They make eye contact with their child and show a facial
expression that, without any words, says, "Stop now, and I mean
business!" Next, directly ask your child what he had planned to do
next. Some children will be shocked to realize that they were about
to hurt someone. They were reacting but not thinking. You then want
to help him evaluate the consequences of his intended action: "What
will happen if you hit Vinny? How will he feel? Is this really what you
want to do?"

You can help your child learn to stop and evaluate her impulses
before she acts by having her imagine a big Stop sign when she feels
angry or frustrated. You can help your child learn this control by
teaching her games that give her practice in literally stopping her
intentions. Here are two suggested games that you may recall from
your own childhood.

Red Light/Green Light

Any number of children can play. All children line up side by
side. One child is chosen to be the "traffic cop." He goes and stands

fifty feet or so in front of the group, and then he turns his back. The traffic cop chants, "Red light, green light, go!" When the traffic cop says "go," the children in the line are to begin running toward the traffic cop. After a few seconds, the traffic cop says, "Red light, green light, stop!" and all the children must stop and freeze very quickly. When the traffic cop says, "stop," he also turns around to face the other players. If the traffic cop spots any of the players moving, they must go back to the starting line. The traffic cop will repeat this pattern of commands in rapid succession. The first player to reach the traffic cop becomes the new traffic cop, and all of the other children return to the starting line.

Statues

There are two versions of this game. In the first version, music is played for the children to dance to; when the music stops, all the children must freeze and hold the position they were in while they were dancing. When a child is caught moving, she is eliminated. The second version is a bit more involved. One person plays the role of an art dealer. This person takes each player by the hands and gently spins them around. When they let go, the player must strike a pose. A second child comes in to look at the statues. He will choose (buy) only a statue that is not moving. The last statue bought becomes the new art dealer or customer.

Alert!

The ability to become less impulsive and to stop and evaluate the consequences of one's behavior has long-lasting benefits. It will help your child manage frustration and improve her social skills while she is young. Having the ability to evaluate choices will also help her later in life to resist peer pressure to engage in risk-taking behaviors such as drug use or gang involvement.

Remembering Rules

A useful technique for helping your child develop self-control is called prompting. When you use prompting, you are stopping your child when you are displeased with his behavior, and asking him to evaluate his actions. Rather than simply reminding your child of a rule or guideline, you are asking him to recall the rule and implications. For example, "What is the rule about hitting?" "What should you do when you are mad at your sister?" "What happens when you leave your toys on the stairs?" Remember to keep your list of rules short and simple. Your young child will genuinely need to be reminded of a rule many times before she will fully internalize it and abide by it. Prompting is an effective way to help your child internalize rules and standards of behavior. Ultimately, your voice of guidance becomes the "little voice" in your child's head.

Thinking Ahead

Once your child has learned to stop his impulsive behavior mid-stream, he is ready to make purposeful choices about his behavior. He is learning to remember rules and predict consequences. Once your child can predict the consequences of a behavior, he will be more able to control his behavior. This will allow your child to plan his response for any given situation.

 **Fact**

Young children have a very limited memory capacity. Before your child is four or five years old, you will need to remind her of the rules, directly and with prompting, many times. When you find yourself saying, "How many times do I have to tell you to___?" try to stay patient and realize that your child is not intentionally forgetting.

Established routines help your child think ahead. Remind your child of routines and set expectations. Slowly you can encourage your child to take some control of routines. Prompting can be very helpful in assisting your child to make appropriate choices within a routine: "What else should you do to get ready for bed?" "What is the first thing you should do when you get home from school? What comes next?"

Coping with Strong Emotions

Just like you, your child is bound to experience strong feelings on occasion. When your child is young, his emotions are very close to the surface and may change rapidly; this can be very overwhelming for him. Some feelings that a young child may have difficulty handling include disappointment, frustration, and anger. Angry feelings range from mild irritation to intense rage. It is important to note that strong feelings often include physiological responses such as a rapid heart rate, muscle tension, or accelerated breathing. These reactions will add to your child's perception of being overwhelmed or out of control.

Accepting Emotions

Having feelings is a hallmark of being human. It is important that you allow and accept all of your child's emotions. On the other hand, you do not have to allow or accept her actions. For example, you might say, "I understand that you are feeling angry, but I cannot permit you to bite Lynda. That is not safe." "It is okay that you feel tired and cranky, but it is not okay for you to throw your food across the room."

Respect your child's feelings and you will help him learn to express and control them appropriately. Avoid discounting your child's emotions. What he is feeling is very real and important to him. You may recall a time when someone patted you on the head and told you, "Don't worry your pretty little head" or "Don't be silly; you should not be so upset." More than likely, you found that a condescending or dismissive response would only flame your already heated emotions. Your child has the right to feel whatever she truly feels. Helping her express that feeling is where you play a part.

Essential

It is tempting to encourage your child to suppress his strong emotions. "Big boys don't cry" is a common adage. We now know this is not good advice. Suppressing emotions does not make them go away. With no safe outlet, bottled-up emotions often are to blame for many adult ailments, everything from headaches to ulcers to heart disease.

Identifying Emotions

A child as young as two years old can start to learn skills for controlling and expressing strong emotions. The first step is for her to be able to identify and label what she is feeling. From the start, make a point of recognizing and labeling your child's feelings for her by saying something like, "Oh, I see you are stomping your feet. I think you are feeling angry." You can prompt your preschooler to identify what emotion she is experiencing: "Trudy, I saw you push Sam. What feeling made you act this way?"

Your child can learn more about her own emotions if you guide her in identifying the emotions of other people. There are specific activities to help your child learn this skill:

- Create flashcards using pictures of people with various facial expressions. Ask your child to label what each person is feeling.
- Use magazine pictures for a project. Ask your child to make a collage of people who look sad, angry, or happy.
- Share a favorite book or movie with your child. Ask her to analyze what a character may be feeling. How did Cinderella feel when she had to stay home from the ball? What do you think Peter Rabbit felt when he was caught in Mr. McGregor's garden?

- Continue the discussion of the story's character by asking your child how she knows how the character is feeling. For example, you might say, "Look at Cinderella's face. How do you think she feels? How can you tell that she feels that way? How would you feel if you had to stay home from the ball?"

Alert!

Recent studies show that preschool-aged children who cannot read and interpret the facial expressions of other children will be more likely to be aggressive once they enter school. There is an early connection between emotional understanding and behavioral problems.

Expressing Emotion

As your child matures, you can teach him specific ways to express his emotions. Your focus is to help your child use words to express how he is feeling. You will find that Chapter 9 is devoted to this topic. Helping your child with verbal expression will give him a sense of control and reduce emotional outbursts and tantrums.

It is also helpful to provide physical outlets for your child. A few ways your child can use her body to express emotions are exercising, dancing, drawing "angry" pictures, or going for a walk.

Learning Problem-Solving Skills

Solving problems is an important skill. Both children and adults meet with problems or conflict almost every day. Some problems your child may face will be small, such as trying to get shoes to fit on a doll. Other problems your child may encounter, such as how to handle a bully, are more complex. If your child learns to solve problems while he is young, he will have a greater sense of control and a higher tolerance for frustration.

 **Fact**

Regardless of the problem, the steps for solving the problem are the same. First, you must correctly identify the problem or the underlying issue. The second step is to brainstorm possible solutions. Next, you evaluate alternatives and possible consequences. Last, you pick a solution to try. If the choice works, you adopt this behavior for similar problems. If the solution does not work, you will try another.

You Are a Role Model

Your child will learn a lot about problem solving by observing you. Imitation is a powerful way to learn. If your child witnesses you calmly and methodically following the steps above, she will be more likely to handle problems the same way.

Consider the following scenario. You and your child have just returned home from a long afternoon of shopping. On the doorstep, you balance your packages as your dig through your purse or pockets for the house key. Your key is gone! Do you lose emotional control and start crying and cursing as your frantically dump out everything onto the porch? Alternatively, do you model appropriate coping and problem-solving skills, sometimes involving your child in the process? For example, you might say, "Oh, dear, the key is lost and we are locked out of the house. Can you help me think of another way to get in? Hmmm, the garage door is locked, too. I need to think of someone else who has a key."

The Impact of Your Response

How you respond when your child has a problem will influence her future problem-solving skills. Imagine that you see that your four-year-old is struggling with a jigsaw puzzle. She is becoming increasingly frustrated with a particular piece and is now on the verge of tears. There are four basic response styles—which is yours?

- **Sensitive.** You say, "Aww, I see you are really upset. Why don't we play with another toy?" This response may make your child feel better but will not help her learn the new skill or how to manage future frustration.
- **Critical.** You say, "Stop crying over that silly puzzle. It is clear that it is too difficult for you." The critical response will only frustrate your child further and will cause her to doubt her own ability or competence.
- **Fixing.** You say, "Oh, look, the red piece needs to . . . never mind, I will finish it for you." This type of response will eliminate the frustration but will only increase your child's dependence on you.
- **Coaching.** You say, "I can see how frustrated you are becoming. What shape do you think you need? What direction can you try with that piece?" The coaching response will encourage your child to manage frustrations and become an independent problem solver.

Avoid the temptation to intervene right away; give your child the opportunity to solve the problem on his own. Sometimes, you can give him a nudge with questions such as, "Do you have an idea?" or "What do you think would happen if you____?" This is the time to brainstorm. Explore even silly or far-fetched ideas. Remember that practice will improve your child's skills.

Problem Solving for Different Age Groups

Even infants and toddlers are beginning to learn how to solve problems. They are learning by direct hands-on exploration. Learning at this age comes from doing, by trial and error. Slowly, your child can see the consequences of his actions. You can see this as he tries to get a round shape into a square hole or a block to balance on its end. By making mistakes, he discovers how to alter his behavior to achieve an intended result. Give your infant or toddler plenty of toys and materials for play and experimentation. Guide him in resolving simple problems such as retrieving a toy that is out of reach.

Essential

Select toys that your child can explore and manipulate to see cause and effect. Some toys good for this are stacking rings, rattles, spinning toys, See 'n Say, or a jack-in-the-box. Toys that can be played with in more than one way, like boxes and blocks, are ideal.

As your child ages, her ability to master problem solving will improve. Advancing verbal skills will aid her negotiation ability. Improved memory capacity will help her recall consequences of her behavior and will aid in learning through imitation. Now your child can try out multiple solutions and compare their effectiveness.

Role-playing is a great way to teach your child how to work through different alternatives. You can engage your preschooler's imagination by using dolls or puppets. Set up a scenario of interest with your child. Play "Let's pretend." Here are some suggestions for possible conflicts: Mr. Frog grabs the block away from Miss Spider, both Piglet and Pooh want the honey pot first, or the three bears find two apples in the forest. Be sure to include a discussion of each of the points of view and of the possible feelings of the characters. Remember to involve your child in generating possible solutions. Encourage your child to script the action. For example, you can ask her, "What can Miss Spider say to Mr. Frog so that she can get the block returned to her?"

Your school-aged child is starting to understand abstract thought. This frees him from trial-and-error learning. He does not have to physically try out multiple solutions; now he can imagine hypothetical situations and outcomes. Help your child develop these skills and learn to analyze and evaluate alternative solutions with the following activities:

Use storybooks as a springboard for a discussion. Identify problems that characters are facing and evaluate how their problems are resolved.

At the top of a large piece of butcher paper, list a potential problem or conflict the child has already experienced. Below, make two columns and title them "Good Choice" and "Bad Choice." Write potential reactions to the problem on index cards and have your child decide where each card belongs. Here is an example problem: You want the puppet that Jimmy is playing with. Here are example reactions: (a) You snatch the toy away from Jimmy, (b) You ask Jimmy for a turn, (c) You find a new toy to play with until Jimmy is done, and (d) You bring a new puppet and ask Jimmy if he wishes to trade.

Helping Your Child Cool Himself Down

The ability to develop skills for self-soothing and self-calming is important. Children and adults who have these skills can handle stress and frustration better than those who don't. You can promote in your child the ability to maintain emotional equilibrium and the ability to roll with the punches. There are strategies appropriate for all ages.

Soothing Young Children

Many young infants and toddlers adopt their own self-soothing behaviors. Thumb sucking may be the earliest example, but other children may rock gently, rub their face with a blanket or other loved object, or twirl their hair. There are many ways you can try to calm your child. Try some of the following to find which works best for your child:

- Play soft music.
- Provide white or droning noise (such as a vacuum).
- Rock your child.
- Stroke or massage your child.

As your child approaches toddlerhood, there are some fun activities that you can use to show your child how to calm herself down. Show her how to relax her body. Ask your child to let her muscles go limp and pretend to be a rag doll. Alternatively, ask her to swirl and twirl scarves in the air. Ask your young child to move like an animal: Stomp through mud like an elephant, fly and glide like a bird, and so forth. These activities force your child to slow down, relax, and move in a calm, controlled manner.

Activities that involve the sense of touch (kinesthetic activities) are often very soothing for young children. Use a bucket or dishpan for a sensory activity. Fill the bucket with water or sand or shaving cream or any tactile material your child may enjoy. Play dough, Gak, Silly Putty, and clay also are very calming materials for your child to manipulate.

 **Essential**

Play dough recipe: Mix ½ cup salt and 1 cup flour together. Add 1 cup water, 1 tablespoon cooking oil, and 1 tablespoon cream of tartar. Heat over low heat and stir. When it clumps up, remove mixture from heat and knead in a few drops of food coloring. Store in an airtight container.

Teaching Skills for Older Children

As your child matures, his ability to calm himself down will improve. Adults as well as children can use many of the activities below. Introduce your child to a variety of strategies and let him discover what works best for him.

Help your child find a special "get away from it all" place. This can be a quiet room in the cellar, a grassy spot under an apple tree, or even just a comfy chair. Any place that he can call his own and where he will be undistracted will work.

Provide opportunities for your child's self-expression. A journal or sketchpad can sometimes help your child vent in a safe way. Provide him with any materials he may need, such as pencils, crayons, and so forth. Be sure to reassure your child that his journal is a private thing for him and that you will not look at it unless he invites you to.

Show your child ways to relax her body with these exercises. Sit quietly, take deep breaths through your nose, and exhale slowly. Try imagining you are breathing through your feet. Listen to the sound of your breath. Curl your body into a tight ball. Slowly uncoil yourself like a cat stretching out. Be sure to slowly stretch as far as you can go. Close your eyes. Focus on one part of your body; clench it tightly. Then relax that part slowly. Imagine it is very loose and heavy. Work from your head to your toes.

 **Fact**

Along with general relaxation, these techniques may result in many other benefits to both adults and children, including improved concentration, memory, and creativity. Additionally, they can help both adults and children manage stress even when they are not directly using these techniques, as they lead to a general sense of calm. Some report that such relaxation techniques improve their sleep and general well-being as well.

Guide your child with creative visualization. You can read or tape scripts for your child to listen to. Here are three to try.

Light as a Feather

Close your eyes and relax. Imagine you are a light little feather. You are dropping slowly from a big white fluffy cloud in the sky. Feel yourself softly sway back and forth. Feel how the wind is pushing you as you glide downward. You are swaying back and forth, back and forth, and back and forth. Feel how a cool breeze makes you tumble through the air. You are slowly descending until you come to a gentle stop on the ground.

At the Beach

You are lying on the warm sand at the beach. You can feel the cool and gritty sand under your back. You feel your feet sinking a bit in the moist sand. You now notice how warm the sun feels on your skin. When you turn your head, you can see all of the tiny crystals of sand, glimmering like diamonds in the sunlight. Take a deep breath; you can smell the warm, salty sea air and the lingering fragrance of suntan lotion. In the distance, you can hear children playing, a gull crying, and the waves crashing on the shore.

In the Forest

You are sitting underneath a great big tree in the middle of the forest. You are resting your back on the hard, rough, and knobby trunk of the tree. You can feel cool spongy moss under your hands as you rest them on the ground. At your feet is a babbling brook. The cool water is splashing up against the rocks and a refreshing spray is hitting your legs. The sunlight is streaming though the leaves and creating a dappled pattern on the forest floor. You close your eyes and you can hear the wind rustling through the leaves and the call of an unknown bird.

CHAPTER 19

When Things Get Out of Control

Temper tantrums are a normal occurrence of childhood. Although some of your child's temper tantrums may be very intense, you will find that they will resolve quickly. On rare occasions, you may find that your child has lost complete control of her emotions and behavior. How do you cope when all of your past tried-and-true calming strategies are not working?

When a Tantrum Continues to Escalate

Most temper tantrums are like summer storms: They arrive with a lot of flash and noise, but they pass fairly quickly. On rare occasions, you may find that your child's temper tantrum is not subsiding as you would expect it to. In fact, it's becoming more intense with each passing moment. Nothing you say or do seems to work, as your child's tantrum continues to escalate.

Who Loses Control?

Toddlers are the most likely to have temper tantrums that escalate. This is because they have very little ability to understand or control their own emotions. Consequently, your child may become overwhelmed or frightened by his strong feelings. Additionally, once in the throes of a temper tantrum, the feeling of being out of control can be very upsetting. You may discover that your child's tantrum has become his response to feeling out of control

and that he has forgotten what triggered his temper tantrum in the first place. Some children will get so worked up that they will urinate or vomit while they are having a temper tantrum. Avoid punishing your child if this happens. It is unintentional. Not only has he lost emotional control, but he has also lost physical control.

Responding When Your Child Is Out of Control

You may have to alter the way that you would normally respond to your child's temper tantrum in this situation. Here are some guidelines. Stay calm. Your child is counting on you to help her regain control. No matter how heated your child's temper becomes, use a calm voice and gentle actions.

Keep her safe. If your child is out of control and thrashing about, you need to take action to prevent her from hurting herself or others. You may even have to pick up your child and move her to a safer place.

Stand back. If your child is completely hysterical, your attempts to distract or calm her may be futile. Your child may be too overwhelmed to listen or think rationally. Wait until after the storm has passed before you attempt to talk about the temper tantrum.

Essential

Sometimes you can stop the trend of rising emotional distress if you can break through your child's hysteria and get his attention. Try flashing the lights off and on, whispering in his ear, or making funny noises.

If You Need to Hold Your Child

There may be times when your child is so out of control that you will need to take dramatic action to keep him safe and secure. When your child is a threat to himself or people nearby, and nothing else works, you can try a "hug hold." Use this technique only as a last resort, and only when you feel calm and in control of your own emotions. Perform a hug hold gently but firmly. Sit behind your child and cross your legs over your child's legs. Reach around the front of your child and hold his arms across his body. Simply let your child know that you are holding him until he is ready to be safe and in control. Hold your child until you feel he has achieved some calm and self-control.

One mother recalls:

> I only had to restrain my son once. He was playing in the cellar with two of his friends from down the street. I don't know what started the incident. All of a sudden, I heard a ruckus and ran down the steps. My son was yelling at his friends about something being unfair. He had taken off his cowboy boots and was trying to hit one of his friends with them. I went over and took his boots away and put them on a shelf. I then tried to sit him down to talk with him. He was so totally out of control that he jumped back and pushed over the chair. He ran over to the shelf, grabbed his boots, and threw them at his friend. He then started to take other things off the shelf and began throwing them. I managed to get behind him and hold on to him. I sat in a chair while I put my legs and arms around him. He was furious. He began screaming at me, "Let me go! Argggh! Let me free!" I tried the best that I could to stay calm and told him that I would hold him until he was in control. He tried to buck back and forth and he tried to spit on my arms! I repeatedly told him that I would hold him safe until he was ready to be in control. Finally, I could feel his body relax and he started to cry. I loosened my hold but still held him until he fully settled down.

Understanding Aggression

Understanding why your child may be aggressive toward others may be difficult. The bottom line is that hurting other people is your child's response to anger or frustration. This is your child's way of expressing these strong emotions. Each child is different; some children are more likely to lash out than others are. There are many factors that may influence your child's aggressive behavior.

Aggression Breeds Aggression

Your child's environment and early experiences will have an impact on her tendency to be aggressive. Research shows that, when young children are exposed to violence or aggression, they are more likely to be aggressive themselves. Your child may be exposed to violence and aggression because she is growing up in a high-crime or war-torn neighborhood. Violence may be close to home and have a stronger impact. In homes where a child is a witness to domestic violence, she observes aggression as a model for emotional expression and conflict resolution.

 **Fact**

Children are very vulnerable, and direct exposure to violence can have a lasting impact. One study found that, if children are first exposed to violence before the age of eleven, they will be three times more likely to develop psychiatric problems than children who are exposed later in life.

Direct exposure to violence affects children differently depending on their age. When young children are exposed to violence, they tend to respond in a more passive way. They may become clingier and show more problems with separation anxiety. They may become generally more fearful and anxious and develop a fear of abandonment. As a result, they may have more nightmares. A younger child may also regress in her behavior and start sucking her thumb or wetting her bed again.

Young children will sometimes act out themes of aggression and violence in their play. By role-playing, they can safely examine and explore their fears while still being in control.

When school-aged children are directly exposed to violence, it will usually affect their behavior. They may become more aggressive and destructive. Alternatively, you may see them become withdrawn and depressed. They will often have difficulty at school as they have problems concentrating. School-aged children may also complain of physical problems such as headaches and stomachaches, and they may become depressed.

Alert!

If you use spanking or any form of physical punishment, your child is more likely to be physically aggressive. This is true even if you are punishing him for aggressive behavior in the first place. To your child, your actions are more influential than your words are, and they send the message, "Do as I do, not as I say."

Types of Aggressive Behavior

There are three main types of aggressive behavior: displaced aggression, instrumental aggression, and hostile aggression. Displaced aggression is when your child's behavior is not directed at the person or object who has angered or frustrated her. This most commonly occurs when your child realizes that she cannot behave aggressively toward the cause of her strong feelings. Perhaps she knows that it would be socially unacceptable, or perhaps she knows that she will get in trouble for doing so. As a result, she takes out her anger or frustration on a safe and more acceptable target. For example, you may see this if Dad has told your child that it's time for her to stop playing and get ready for bed. She is angry and frustrated with Dad, but she knows that she cannot yell back at him. She enters the house crying and whining, then kicks the dog.

Using aggression as a means to a goal is called instrumental aggression. For example, your child may push someone out of the way to get a seat closer to the television. Instrumental aggression will decrease as your child matures and becomes less impulsive. Hostile aggression, on the other hand, tends to occur more frequently as children grow older. Hostile aggression is when your child intentionally sets out to harm someone else. Children who are most likely to use hostile aggression tend to have or mistrustful demeanor and outlook. They tend to lash out in either self-defense or retaliation at those who they perceive (realistically or not) will or have hurt them.

The Role of Television

There is no longer any doubt: Countless research studies have shown that violent content on TV influences a child's aggressive behavior. The impact is greater on children with emotional, behavioral, or impulse-control problems. Additionally, children are more likely to imitate the behaviors in shows in which the violence is particularly realistic or in which the aggressor goes unpunished or is rewarded. It does not seem to matter if the show is animated or live action.

In addition to leading him to imitate what he sees, viewing violent and aggressive acts on TV can have other effects on your child. Studies show that the child who views violent programming may begin to accept aggression as a way to solve problems. He will also become desensitized to acts of violence and aggression. These children will display an increased level of fearfulness and mistrust.

 **Fact**

Children spend an average of twenty-three hours a week watching TV. The average child will spend more time watching TV than he will spend in school. Guidelines from the American Academy of Pediatrics recommend that children under the age of two should not watch TV at all, and older children should be limited to less than two hours a day.

Realistically, it is probably not feasible or even desirable to completely ban your child from watching television. Therefore, it is wise for you to monitor closely and limit what your child watches on TV. Take advantage of TV program rating guides or the V chip. Whenever possible, work with your child to discuss and plan appropriate viewing choices.

Watch questionable shows with your child. Look for opportunities to discuss and evaluate aggressive or violent behaviors. You can ask her questions such as, "Can you think of a better way the Power Rangers could have solved that problem?" "Could that really happen?" "Why do you think there is so much fighting?" You can also help children see the difference between fact and fantasy by saying something like, "In real life, that coyote would not be able to walk after falling off of the cliff."

The Role of Toys

Play is the most powerful vehicle for young children's learning. When your young child plays, he is exploring and discovering the world around him. Children learn best through direct hands-on experience, and play is the way children do this. If play is your child's work, then toys are his tools. The toys that you provide will directly influence the tone and direction of your child's play. For example, balls and hula hoops will promote active play, and books and puzzles will promote quiet play.

Good toys are safe and age appropriate. They encourage your child to be creative, curious, or cooperative. Good toys will encourage your child to explore and problem solve. Toys that can be played with in many ways are best. These are called open-ended toys and include dolls, blocks, puppets, and Legos.

Bad toys are ones that are very limiting in regard to how a child can play with them. There are not many diverse play themes a child can explore with the "Gomaimem" action figure. Violent toys send violent messages. Toy weapons and violent action figures are among the toys that encourage children to reenact the aggression they see on TV.

 **Fact**

> One year after the FCC deregulated children's TV, seven out of ten of the best-selling toys were connected to a violent children's show. One survey found that 91 percent of teachers report seeing more violent behavior as a result of tie-in marketing of toys and other licensed products.

The Development of Aggression

Although it is believed that we are born with the potential for both caring and violence, it is important to note that specific aggressive behavior is influenced and shaped by environment and experiences.

Infant and Toddler Aggression

Your infant's earliest aggressive actions are not intentional. Your infant may grab your face or pull the hair of a playmate. Your child's genuine curiosity and exploration usually cause these behaviors. Your child will not understand how her actions harm another person, so even her rough-and-tumble or playful advances can get out of hand.

Your infant will not understand being punished for these behaviors, but you can take advantage of a teachable moment. Make it clear from the start that aggressive behavior will not be allowed. Even "cute" behaviors such as playful smacks and love bites should be discouraged. Moreover, remember that you are your child's primary role model!

Sometimes your child may accidentally hurt another child or family pet with his "friendly" advances. If this happens, gently stop your child. You can even take his hand to show him how to hug or pet gently while saying, "You are hurting the kitty. Here is how to pet her. See how soft and gentle your touch must be?" Realize that you may need to do this many times.

You can expect your child to display feelings of anger and frustration somewhere between nine and twelve months of age. There are many reasons why children this age will express themselves with aggressive actions.

- They lack the ability to express their emotions or desires with words.
- They have poor impulse control.
- They cannot manage their strong emotions.
- They are egocentric.

Most aggression during the toddler years is instrumental aggression. Toddlers are learning how their behavior can influence someone. Aggressive behavior always gets a reaction, and often it will get the child what she wants: "If I bite Timmy, he will let go of the toy that I want." If your toddler is often hurting others, you may need to make the extra effort to closely supervise her. Stop your child's aggression. Patiently show her how to appropriately express herself with words. You may tell her something like, "Pinching hurts! If you are angry, tell Sylvia, 'Stop, I am mad!'"

 Essential

There is a relationship between gender and aggression. Boys do tend to be more aggressive, although it is hard sometimes to determine whether testosterone, cultural acceptance, or media role models has the largest impact.

Preschool Aggression

As your child approaches preschool age, his ability to tolerate frustration will improve, and he will have stronger language skills and impulse control. Overall, the presence of aggression during temper tantrums should decline as his self-control develops. However, your child may still experience complete meltdowns and possibly hurt others in the process. Try to quickly stop your child's aggression by redirecting or prompting. You can try to encourage him to use words to solve the problem. If all else fails, you will need to remove him from anyone he could hurt. You may need to help him sit in time-out so that he can regain his composure and self-control.

Your preschooler is starting to show an understanding of right and wrong. Early moral development is characterized by decisions that are made according to how their outcome will affect the child. In other words, in the child's eyes, right and acceptable actions are those that help her avoid punishment or gain a reward: "It is wrong to hit the cat because then it will scratch me."

School-Age Aggression

You should expect to see a noticeable decline in aggression from your child by the time he enters school. By now, he should be showing an indication that he is socialized to internalize society's conduct rules and standards. The school-ager is now showing that he has a conscience. His moral thought and decision making are influenced by the opinions of peers and the rules set by authority figures. He would say, "It is wrong to hit the cat because my friends will think I am a bully."

 **Question?**

What is objective morality?
Described by psychologist Jean Piaget, it is the view that your child judges good or bad behavior based on the result of the action, rather than the motivation. From this perspective, the naughtier child is the one who broke four glasses by accident, not the child who smashed one heirloom vase on purpose.

Responding to Aggression

Although there are times when it is wise to ignore a tantrum, you must respond promptly when your child is aggressive. You need to make it clear that it is never acceptable to hurt herself or someone else. In contrast, be sure to communicate that you accept your child's feelings. It is okay to be angry, sad, irritated, and so forth. You may say something like, "I can understand why you are angry that you have to come inside, but I will not let you hurt the dog." You may wish to add, "There are better ways to show your anger." (See suggestions for managing destructive behaviors later in this chapter.) This way, you are rejecting the behavior, not your child's feelings.

Punishment is rarely an effective way to respond to aggression. Often, punishment only creates anger and resentment, which may lead to further aggression. Your goal is to use positive discipline to help your child learn appropriate ways to express her strong emotions. You can read more about punishment and discipline in Chapter 5.

Essential

It is worthwhile to help your child learn the difference between aggressive behavior and assertive behavior. Giving up aggressive behavior does not mean that he has to be passive and give up everything he wants. Assertive behavior means standing up for your own desires and rights while protecting the desires and rights of the other person.

When your child hurts someone, focus your attention on the victim. This sends the message to your child that aggression is not an effective way to get what she wants. You can also use this as an opportunity to show your child how her behavior affects someone else: "Can you see that Jacob is crying? He is upset because you took his toy train away from him while he was playing."

When Your Child Hurts Himself

There may be times while your child is having a temper tantrum that he could be at risk for hurting himself. Most of the time, the injury will be unintentional, resulting from flailing on the floor or accidentally hitting himself. It is always a good idea to stay close to younger children when they are having a temper tantrum, to help keep them safe.

Intentional Harm

Some young children will intentionally hurt themselves during a temper tantrum. These children become so overwrought with frustration anger that they bite themselves or pull their own hair. If your child is truly hurting herself, you will need to intervene. If you cannot distract or redirect her behavior, then you may need to use the hug hold described above. Be sure to remind your child, "I'm not going to let you hurt yourself."

 **Fact**

Although rare, sometimes young children will intentionally harm themselves in a calm, more methodical fashion. They may intentionally burn or cut themselves. This behavior is discussed in Chapter 20.

Additionally, your child may engage in head banging or breath holding. These are also intentional behaviors. These are very dramatic behaviors that your child has learned are effective in getting your attention.

Head Banging

Head banging is a behavior that can occur anywhere from nine months to two years of age. Up to 20 percent of all children will head bang. Boys are more likely than girls are to engage in this behavior. If you witness your child banging his head, you will understandably be distraught, although most children do not bang their head hard enough to truly hurt themselves. Your instinct will probably be to pick up your child and comfort him to get him to stop. Consequently, you are inadvertently reinforcing the behavior.

Head banging can, on rare occasion, be a symptom of a psychiatric or neurological disorder. It is a good idea to alert your pediatrician when you first observe this behavior. If it is found that your child's head banging is a temper tantrum behavior, then you can work together to find ways to keep your child safe without creating a fuss. Perhaps this means that you will make sure that your child is safe and then ignore him as you would when he is having a full-blown attention-seeking temper tantrum.

Breath Holding

Although also not a harmful behavior, breath holding is perhaps the most frightening common, benign behavior of childhood. Many parents don't realize how common breath holding is. Approximately 5 percent of all children will have breath-holding spells, and they may occur anytime between the ages of one and four. One mother shares, "My son would get angry and just stand and hold his breath . . . . not a sound was coming from him. His lips would turn blue and I would hold him so he would not fall. As soon as he went limp, then he would take a deep breath and begin to scream."

Alert!

The first time your child has a breath-holding spell, you should take your child to the doctor to rule out any possible physical causes. As with head banging, children can learn to hold their breath for attention. If there is no physical cause, your doctor will probably advise that you try not to reinforce the behavior.

When a child has a breath-holding spell, she will hold her breath until she turns blue and passes out. Some children will also have a small seizure. The good news is that these spells resolve spontaneously.

Soon after the child passes out, she will start to breathe, usually within one or two minutes.

When Your Child Is Destructive

While in the throes of a major temper tantrum, your child may throw or break things. This may be accidental or intentional. As your child is thrashing about, he could easily knock over or hit something. If you predict that your child's temper tantrum will be this out of control, you should secure the area around him as much as you can.

There are times when you may see your child being intentionally destructive. Perhaps he is marking walls or breaking toys at times when he seems to be emotionally in control, but he may still be acting on strong emotions. If your child is destructive with toys, reconsider their appropriateness for your child's age. It may be that your child is too young, and the toy's complexity is frustrating him. Alternatively, if your child is too old for the toy, he will find it boring.

Many activities can help your child channel his destructive impulses. Here are just a few:

- Shred scraps of paper
- Kick a pillow around
- Pull weeds
- Throw rolled socks into a basket
- Scribble hard on the sidewalk with chalk

The way that you should respond to your child's destructive behavior does not depend on whether you believe your child's actions were intentional or not. With your toddler, try redirection. Show her a more appropriate option. For example, "If you wish to cut with the scissors, use them for cutting paper instead of the baby doll's pretty hair." If your child is older, you can also use logical consequences. This is when you require your child to take responsibility for his actions. If he paints on the table, he must clean it off. If he tears a book, he must repair it with clear Con-Tact paper.

CHAPTER 20

When to Be Concerned

Y ou thought that you were ready for any behavior that your child might throw your way. In fact, you expected that you would see your child throw some temper tantrums along the way. However, you did not expect to see your child have such intense behavior problems. Your child's behavior appears to be more extreme and problematic than that of any other child you know. When should you start to worry? Should you be concerned that your child has developmental or conduct problems?

What Is Normal for Your Child's Age?

Temper tantrums are a normal behavior that you can expect to see as your child develops. Although you may be concerned that your child's tantrum behavior is not normal, odds are that it is.

Your knowledge of how children behave is probably based, for the most part, on your interactions with your own children. You can reasonably expect that, if you have more than one child, each one will be different. Perhaps your two older children have calm dispositions and rarely had temper tantrums. When your third child displays defiance and a stormier demeanor, it is important to remember that her behavior may still be well within the realm of normal. You may find it helpful if you can objectively gauge what are common expectations of behavior for the age of your child. You can gain a wider and less biased perspective in a few ways.

Review Your Expectations

The question is not whether you perceive your child's behavior to be normal, but whether it is normal in comparison to that of other children her age. Take time to observe your child when she is playing and interacting with other children her own age. Stand back, watch, listen, and ask yourself these questions:

- Is she generally well liked and accepted by the other children?
- Does she seem to tolerate frustration as well as the other children do?
- Is she equal with the other children in problem solving and conflict resolution?
- Can she manage and control her strong emotions as well as the other children her age do?

If you answer no to any of these items, you may wish to investigate further the root of your child's difficulties.

Other parents with children in the same age range as yours can be a wonderful support and resource. Take time to compare notes and share strategies. You may find that you are not so troubled by your toddler's mealtime meltdowns when you hear that Timmy's mother is dealing with this very same issue! Additionally, Amber's mother may have found a great way to cope with sharing conflicts that will work well for you, too.

Question?

How old is too old for a temper tantrum?
Even adults will have their forms of temper tantrums from time to time. Toddlerhood is prime time for temper tantrums. You should not see your child's tantrums worsening after the age of four. Five to 10 percent of five- and six-year-olds will still have daily temper tantrums, but both their frequency and intensity should continue to decrease.

You can also gain valuable insight from other sources. Books like the one you are reading now can help you learn what is normal and expected behavior for your child's age and development level. If your child is in school or child care, it may be worthwhile to share your concerns with your child's teacher or provider. He or she may be able to offer valuable insight because he or she will have knowledge of child development theory and your individual child's temperament and behavior.

Intensity

If you are still concerned about your child's temper tantrum behavior, look at the intensity of his temper tantrums. As there are many different things that may trigger a temper tantrum in your child, your child will exhibit many different ways of responding. Normally, the intensity of your child's tantrum should reflect the level of his emotions. For example, your child may scream and kick when her favorite new toy falls to the ground and breaks, but you should see less intensity in her response when she drops a cookie and it breaks. What you should not see is a child who often overreacts to the smallest of disappointments and frustration.

If you end up walking on eggshells, awaiting the next trigger that will send your child into a rage, you should be concerned. You also do not want to see your child having atypical emotional responses. For example, if your child often cries when you would expect him to be happy, or laughs or seems joyous when he experiences or sees something sad, you should be concerned.

Additionally, the level of intensity of your child's tantrum will influence your ability to console or comfort her; if you find that you are constantly having difficulty in helping your child regain control, you may have cause for concern. With your intervention, most temper tantrums should wind down within five minutes. You will, on occasion, witness an outburst that lasts longer, but you should not see temper tantrums that frequently last for more than fifteen minutes.

Too Many Tantrums?

The number and frequency of your child's temper tantrums will vary, influenced by factors such as stress and your child's level of maturity. During the toddler years, you may see your child have more than one tantrum in a day. The good news is that the frequency of your child's outbursts should begin to decrease noticeably by the time he is around four years old. Some experts recommend that you should alert your pediatrician if your child never has any temper tantrums at all. At any age, more than three temper tantrums a day, over a period of more than a few days, is not normal.

Is Your Child Too Aggressive?

Some amount of aggressive behavior is common when your child is having a temper tantrum. While she is struggling with strong feelings of anger and frustration, she may lash out and hurt someone. If you have reason for concern regarding your child's temper tantrums, odds are that aggression plays a role in your concerns. You can learn to identify when your child's aggressive behavior has crossed the line.

There are three basic levels of aggression/violence. The first level is mainly instrumental aggression. This includes behaviors such as pushing, grabbing, and restraining another child. In the second level, the behavior is more intentional, and you may see your child slap, pinch, kick, or hit. The behaviors associated with the third level are violent and are always cause for concern. These behaviors include choking, hitting with an object, using weapons, and not stopping when the victim protests.

Although the focus here is on aggressive behaviors that occur during temper tantrums, there are other signs that can indicate to you that your child has an ongoing or potential problem with violence. If your child gets in lots of fights or your child threatens or intimidates children who are younger or weaker, you should be concerned. When there is a problem, child care providers, teachers, or other parents will often complain about your child's aggression. You should be worried if your child is cruel to animals. Your child may act aggressively with little or no provocation and other children will start to avoid or reject your child because of his aggressive behavior.

Essential

Most forms of aggression should decrease over time. Instrumental aggression usually decreases as children mature and gain verbal skills. Intentionally aggressive behaviors should also decrease once your child learns more appropriate ways to resolve conflict and express anger.

If your child is overly aggressive or violent, he may show a preoccupation with violence and violent content. You may see them depict graphically violent images in their artwork. They may be preoccupied with violent television shows or video games as well. Please note: Some degree of power/superhero play is normal for young children. The key is that you want to see them play and interact with other children in many ways without always resorting to aggression or violent themes.

Red Flags in Behavior

Temper tantrums alone are usually not alarming or a cause for concern. However, if your child is also exhibiting any of the behaviors described below, it may be wise to seek out a professional evaluation for your child.

Changes in Habits

Stress and emotional upheaval often result in changes in your child's sleep and/or eating habits. You may see a rapid increase or decrease in your child's appetite or eating patterns. One mother shares:

I felt comfortable that my son was adjusting well to day care. He was always eager to go, he never experienced any separation anxiety, and he was enthusiastic to tell me what he did there at the end of the day. After about two weeks at day care, he suddenly stopped eating breakfast. The first day I questioned his health, but he said he felt fine, and his teacher said he ate well at day care. The second day, I chalked it up to fussiness, as he seemed happy and had no other complaints or symptoms. By the end of the week, it became apparent that his appetite had fallen off at dinnertime, too. My son insisted he felt well and that nothing was bothering him. It was only on the following Monday, when I called his day care, that I learned that he was very upset because his favorite teacher had told his class that she would be leaving for a new school.

Nightmares are common in childhood and can be particularly troublesome for the child who has difficulty distinguishing between fact and fantasy. However, if your child's nightmares are becoming more persistent, your child may be under stress and distress.

Changes in Demeanor

Your child may be troubled and may benefit from professional help if you observe changes in her social or emotional demeanor. Has she recently become exceedingly fearful or anxious? Is she exhibiting low self-esteem? Has she become sullen or withdrawn lately? Has she regressed (gone backward) in her behavior or development? For example, your three-year-old suddenly insists on drinking from a bottle, or your seven-year-old begins to wet the bed at night.

Self-Injury

It is likely that there will be a time that your child will hurt herself. This may occur when she is flailing about on the floor or kicking and swinging at things around her. This is very different from self-injurious behavior. Self-injurious behavior is when your child is deliberately hurting himself without intending to commit suicide. You should alert a doctor or mental health professional if you believe your child is intentionally hurting himself.

Alert!

Self-injurious behavior may be difficult for you to detect. Children usually feel shame and embarrassment about the behavior; therefore, they often harm themselves only when they are alone.

Although there are many ways that your child may choose to hurt herself, some behaviors are much more common than others. The top three are:

- Carving or cutting the skin with a sharp object
- Burning or branding with cigarettes or matches
- Biting

Girls are more likely to injure themselves, possibly because they are more likely to turn aggressive impulses inward rather than expressing them openly. Experts believe that the child who self-injures is doing so to release strong emotions and reduce tension. Some children self-injure so that they can feel pain and combat feelings of detachment. Other children may harm themselves due to feelings of worthlessness, hopelessness, or guilt.

Autism

Extreme and uncontrollable temper tantrums are one of the signs of autism. Both public concern and information about autism have grown in the last twenty years. Autism is a developmental disorder. Each child with autism will be affected differently. The range of symptoms and behaviors occurs on a broad spectrum. Some children may be disabled while others may be fully functional and independent.

 **Fact**

> The signs of autism are usually observed in children ages one to three. Fifteen out of every 10,000 children will have this disorder. Boys are four times as likely as girls are to be diagnosed with autism.

Most children with autism are diagnosed around age two or three, though diagnoses around and before age two are now being made a little more frequently as a result of the research that has identified preverbal red flags. Social and communicative characteristics that may be red flags for autism in very young infants include lack of eye contact, lack of interest in caregivers during what would ordinarily be considered pleasurable interactions (i.e., feeding), and lack of early social reciprocity and affective responses to interaction (mirroring movement, affect, facial expression, and vocalizations).

Autistic Temper Tantrums

There are some key ways in which autism temper tantrums are different than normal tantrums. All in all, the autistic child's temper tantrums are more intense than average temper tantrums are, and it will take longer for adults to console the child and help the child to regain control. When an autistic child has a temper tantrum, it is often difficult to identify the cause. Instead of being able to say, "Okay, he is having a meltdown because I won't buy him candy" or "She is having a temper tantrum because she is tired," the reasons for this child's temper tantrum may seem completely arbitrary. Temper tantrums in the autistic child are very unpredictable. There is often no set pattern, characteristics, or responses. The very same trigger may result in various scenarios. One morning, your child may find that his cereal is too soggy and will sob uncontrollably. The next day, your child, again finding soggy cereal, will scream obscenities and throw his cereal bowl across the room.

Communication Difficulties

Although autism manifests itself in many ways, many children with autism will exhibit communication difficulties. Experts recommend that your child be evaluated if you agree with any of the following items:

- Your child does not babble or coo by her first birthday.
- Your child does not gesture or wave by her first birthday.
- Your child has not said his first word by the age of sixteen months.
- Your child has not said a two-word phrase by his second birthday.
- Your child has exhibited a loss or regression of language skills.

Other Indications of Autism

There are a wide range of other behaviors that could possibly indicate that your child is autistic. However, seeing one behavior does not automatically mean that your child has autism. There may be a separate isolated reason for a behavior. For example, one warning sign is diminished eye contact, which may also indicate vision or hearing difficulties.

Autistic children are often withdrawn from others and from their surroundings. Along with diminished eye contact, they may ignore verbal interactions. Some children show echolalia. That is, rather than responding to what someone says to him, the child echoes it back, often repeating it multiple times. The autistic child may also withdraw physically. She may resist being touched. Additionally, autistic children often have difficulty playing or interacting with other children.

The autistic child may exhibit an extreme version of the adaptability temperament trait. Adaptability is discussed in detail in Chapter 2. Autistic children may be very slow to adapt, insisting on sameness and routine. They react very strongly to any change in their daily life. Something as minor as forgetting to cut the crust off their peanut butter and jelly sandwich may lead to a temper tantrum.

Essential

Self-stimulation behaviors (repetitive physical actions) such as rocking, spinning, and head banging are commonly seen in children with autism. However, be aware that these behaviors are also seen in children who are experiencing a lot of stress in their lives.

Attention Deficit Hyperactivity Disorder

Jason is a bundle of energy. He is always on the go, flitting from one activity to another. He has temper tantrums at the drop of a hat, particularly when he is asked to sit still or wait quietly. Does this describe a child with attention deficit hyperactivity disorder (ADHD) or an average preschool-aged child? It is often difficult to tell, as behaviors associated with ADHD are often normal for young children.

As many as 40 percent of parents will, at some time, suspect that their child has ADHD. The reality is that only 10 percent of children are diagnosed with ADHD. Furthermore, children under the age of six are rarely diagnosed. It is believed the reason for this disparity is due to a heightened awareness of the disorder, along with generally higher parental expectations.

Could Your Child Have ADHD/ADD?

You can have a more objective perspective on whether your child needs to be evaluated for ADHD if you educate yourself about what are reasonable behaviors and expectations for your child's age. It is likely that your child exhibits some of the behaviors described below. What you need to ask yourself is, "Is my child having more difficulty than other children his age?"

A father tells about a morning with his daughter who has ADHD:

> She is constantly on the go. This morning was no different. She would barely sit at the table long enough to eat breakfast. Soon

afterward, she was upstairs bouncing on her bed. I started up the stairs to remind her that she is not allowed to do that but she met me halfway as she was sliding down the steps on her bottom. She went back up the steps and all was quiet for ten or fifteen minutes. Then I heard some loud banging. When I went to her room, I found her sitting in a pile of yarn and craft materials crying. Over in the corner I could see one of the many projects that she had started tossed in the corner where she had three or four unfinished drawings. "What's wrong, baby?" I asked her. She yelled back at me, "I'm bored, bored, bored!" and she got up and kicked all the yarn under the bed. I sat in the rocker and patted my knee. "Come sit with me," I called. She came over and sat on my lap, but as soon as I tried to put my arm around her, she squirmed off and ran down the steps. By the time I caught up with her, she was doing somersaults over the back of the couch.

 *Essential*

Attention deficit disorder (ADD) generally has two main behavioral components: difficulty paying attention and impulsiveness. When a child with ADD is also hyperactive, he is said to have ADHD.

Temper tantrums may be common in children with ADHD/ADD as they will often be very impulsive and have difficulty delaying gratification. This may make tasks like waiting for a turn and sharing quite hard. The child with ADHD/ADD may have temper tantrums that last longer than average, but they will usually resolve within twenty to thirty minutes. It is important to note that most misbehaviors on the part of a child with ADHD/ADD are unintentional. For example, she may frequently be destructive, but this comes from careless rather than spiteful actions.

The child with ADHD will have difficulty paying attention. He may have a hard time completing a task, or he may be very careless in finishing a project. He does not pay attention to detail. These children can be observed starting many activities at once without following though on them. Easily distracted, they may leave behind many half-read books and partially built block towers. Being easily distracted also means the child will have a hard time listening, and he will often appear to be forgetful. You may be frustrated with him for always losing things.

Children with ADHD are often very impulsive. They will often interrupt others to add to a conversation. They may want to jump ahead in a line, and they may have a hard time playing a game that requires that they wait for their turn. Your child may have difficulty sitting still. When he must sit still, you will often see him squirm or fidget. He may talk excessively and be always on the move.

At Home with ADHD

Whether or not your child's pediatrician has chosen to put your child on medication, there are some concrete ways that you can help her manage.

- **Make a special place for her.** Because your child is easily distracted, completed tasks in a timely fashion may prove to be difficult. Set aside a workspace for your child. Remove as many distractions as you can. Have her desk face the wall. Remove the radio and TV from her work area.
- **Help keep your child on task.** You can help your child by prompting him: "Okay, you have folded the socks, now what should you do?" Break down complicated chores or tasks into smaller pieces. Instead of telling him to clean out the garage, give him one small task at a time, such as, "Go and put all the toys in the garage in the big box that is in there. Then report back to me." If your child is a visual learner, try drawing him a diagram for the steps that he needs to take.

- **Help your child get organized.** Children with ADHD often flourish with a lot of structure and routine. It helps them when there is predictability and order in their lives. Help them keep their time organized with to-do lists and calendars. There are many closet organizers and products that you can use to help your child keep her belongs together and organized.
- **Get her attention.** Do not assume that she heard you when you called to her from the backyard. Call her name, get down on her level, and make eye contact before speaking with her.
- **Let him move.** If your child needs to move, give him opportunities to move. If you can, dedicate a space indoors where he can dance or exercise safely, and try to plan outdoor playtime every day, weather permitting. You can add physical activity to everyday activities. Perhaps suggest to your child that he "hop like a bunny" on his way to the bathroom.

Other Concerns

Temper tantrums alone do not indicate that your child has a problem. There are, however, disorders that include temper tantrums as one of the indicators.

Oppositional Defiant Disorder

Oppositional defiant disorder (ODD) is sometimes recognized in young children. It is marked by a persistent pattern of behavior where the child is very negative, hostile, and defiant. At least four of the listed signs must be present in your child's behavior for longer than six months in order for your child to be diagnosed with ODD. It is important for you to realize that these behaviors go well beyond the limit-testing behaviors that are typical for toddlers seeking autonomy or for teenagers making a bid for their independence. Here are some of the signs of ODD: argues with adults, often loses his temper, refuses to comply with adult requests or rules, generally angry and resentful, deliberately annoys people, blames others for her mistakes or misbehavior, touchy and easily annoyed by others, often appears spiteful or vindictive.

It is recommended that all adults involved in this child's care and supervision work together. You should all have a system of open communication and present a united front to the child. This is because the child with ODD will often blame others (including other adults) for her behavior. Agree how each problem will be handled in advance so that you are prepared to react in a calm, unemotional fashion.

If you suspect that your child has ODD, you should contact your pediatrician. In the meantime, what seems to work best for these children is a form of behavior modification. Simply put, this means that you will focus on, recognize, and reinforce the positive behaviors that your child engages in. You can set up a reward or token system as explained in Chapter 5.

Bipolar Disorder

Bipolar disorder, sometimes also called manic depression, is identified in children who exhibit extreme and sometimes rapid changes in mood, energy, thinking, or behavior.

In general, the child with bipolar disorder will appear very moody, swinging between bouts of depression and mania, a state of heightened mood and energy. The bipolar child may be very impulsive at times. Sometimes she will be very motivated and eager, while at other times she will be lethargic and apathetic. The child with bipolar disorder may have explosive temper tantrums, and she may be prone to strong separation anxiety. Tantrums may be particularly intense when the child is in a manic state, as the child is releasing both physical and emotional energy. Bipolar tantrums can last for hours, and some children will lose their memory of having had them. These tantrums will be even more trying for you than a normal tantrum would be. Keep in mind that there is a reason why your child is having such difficulty controlling her emotions and behavior. Your own calm and patience will go a long way toward calming the storm.

Further Resources

Books for Young Children

Adoff, Arnold. *Black Is Brown Is Tan.* (Harper & Row, 1992)

Agassi, Martine, Heinlen, Marieka (Illustrator). *Hands Are Not for Hitting.* (Free Spirit, 2002)

Aliki. *Feelings.* (Mulberry Books, 1985)

Ancona, George. *Helping Out.* (Clarion, 1985)

Bang, Molly. *When Sophie Gets Angry—Really, Really Angry.* (Scholastic, 1999)

Berenstain, Stan, Berenstain, Jan. *Berenstain Bears Get the Gimmies.* (Random House, 1988)

Breeze, L., Morris, A. *This Little Baby's Bedtime.* (Little, Brown, 1990)

Brown, Tricia. *Someone Special, Just Like You.* (Henry Holt, 1991)

Carlson, Nancy. *How to Lose All Your Friends.* (Puffin, 1977)

Clifton, L. *My Friend Jacob.* (Elsevier/Dutton, 1980)

Crary, Elizabeth, Megale, Marina (Illustrator). *I Want It.* (Parenting Press, 1996)

Crary, Elizabeth, Whitney, Jean (Illustrator). *I'm Frustrated (Dealing with Feelings Series).* (Parenting Press, 1992)

Emberley, Ed E., Miranda, Anne (Illustrator). *Glad Monster, Sad Monster: A Book about Feelings.* (Little, Brown & Company, 1997)

Everitt, Betsy. *Mean Soup.* (Harcourt Brace & Company, 1995)

Fassler, J. *Howie Helps Himself.* (Whitman, 1975)

Formby, Caroline. *Tristan's Temper Tantrum.* (Child's Play International, Ltd., 1996)

Fox, Mem. *Harriet, You'll Drive Me Wild!* (Harcourt Children's Books, 2000)

French, Vivian, Elgar, Rebecca (Illustrator). *Tiger and the Temper Tantrum.* (Houghton Mifflin, 1999)

Kingsley, Emily Perl. *I Can Do It Myself.* (Western, 1980)

Lachner, Dorothea, Thong, Khing (Illustrator). *Andrew's Angry Words.* (North-South Books, 1997)

Little, Lessie Jone, Greenfield, Eloise. *I Can Do It by Myself.* (Thomas Y. Crowell, 1978)

Mayer, Mercer. *There's a Nightmare in My Closet.* (Puffin Books, 1976)

Miller, Margaret. *Baby Faces.* (Simon & Schuster, 1998)

Minarik, Else Holmelund, Sendak, Maurice (Illustrator). *No Fighting No Biting.* (Harper Trophy, 1978)

Parr, Todd. *Feelings Book.* (Little, Brown & Company, 2000)

Preston, Edna Mitchel. *The Temper Tantrum Book.* (Penguin Putnam Books for Young Readers, 1971)

Spelman, Cornelia Maude, Cote, Nancy. *When I Feel Angry.* (Albert Whitman, 2000)

Spier, Peter. *People.* (Doubleday, 1980)

Steptoe, John. *Daddy Is a Monster . . . Sometimes.* (Harper & Row, 1983)

Stevenson, Harvey (Illustrator). *The Chocolate-Covered-Cookie Tantrum.* (Houghton Mifflin, 1999)

Viorst, Judith. *Good-Bye Book.* (Simon & Schuster, 1992)

Books for Older Children

Anderson, Penny S., Siculan, Dan (Illustrator). *Feeling Frustrated.* (Scholastic Library Publishing, 1983)

Anfousse, Ginette. *Arthur Throws a Tantrum.* (Formac, 1993)

Brown, Marc. *How to Be a Friend: A Guide to Making Friends and Keeping Them.* (Little, Brown, 2001).

Burnett, Karen Gedig, Barrows, Laurie (Illustrator). *Simon's Hook: A Story about Teases and Put Downs.* (GR Publishing, 1999)

Cohen-Posey, Kate, Lampe, Betsy A. (Illustrator). *How to Handle Bullies, Teasers and Other Meanies: A Book That Takes the Nuisance out of Name Calling and Other Nonsense.* (Rainbow Books, 1995)

Crary, Elizabeth, Whitney, Jean (Illustrator). *I'm Frustrated (Dealing with Feelings Series).* (Parenting Press, 1992)

Kay, Barbara, Polland, Kay, Deroy, Craig (Illustrator). *We Can Work It Out: Conflict Resolution for Children.* (Ten Speed Press, 2000)

Lichtenheld, Tom. *What Are You So Grumpy About?* (Little, Brown, 2003)

Lite, Lori, Hartigan, Meg (Illustrator). *Boy and a Bear: The Children's Relaxation Book.* (Specialty Press, 1996)

Madison, Lynda, Bendell, Norm (Illustrator). *Feelings Book: The Care and Keeping of Your Emotions.* (Pleasant Company Publications, 2002)

McDonald, Megan. *The Judy Moody Mood Journal.* (Candlewick, 2003)

Moser, Adolph. *Don't Rant and Rave on Wednesdays! The Children's Anger-Control Book.* (Landmark Editions, 1994)

Romain, Trevor. *Cliques, Phonies, and Other Baloney.* (Free Spirit Publishing, 1998)

Spinelli, Jerry. *Loser.* (HarperCollins, 2003)

Verdick, Elizabeth, Lisovskis, Marjorie. *How to Take the Grrrr out of Anger.* (Free Spirit, 2002)

Webster-Doyle, Terrence. *Why Is Everybody Always Picking on Me? A Guide to Understanding Bullies for Young People.* (Weatherhill, 1999)

Books for Parents

Ames, Louise Bates, Ilg, Frances L., Haber, Carol C. *Your Two-Year-Old: Terrible or Tender.* (Dell, 1997)

Bailey, Becky A., Ph.D. *Easy to Love, Difficult to Discipline.* (Morrow & Co., 2000)

Barnes, Robert G. *Who's in Charge Here?: Overcoming Power Struggles with Your Kids.* (Word, 1990)

Bettelheim, Bruno. *Love Is Not Enough.* (Avon Books, 1950)

Bowlby, John. *Attachment and Loss. Vol. 1: Attachment.* (Basic Books, 1969)

Brazelton, T. Berry. *Touchpoints: Your Child's Emotional and Behavioral Development.* (Addison-Wesley, 1992)

Craig, Judi, Ph.D. *Parents on the Spot: What to Do When Kids Put You There.* (Hearst Books, 1994)

Cuthbertson, J., Schevill, S. *Helping Your Child Sleep Through the Night.* (Doubleday, 1985)

Dobson, James C. *The Strong-Willed Child.* (Tyndale House, 1992)

Eisenberg, Arlene, Markoff, Heidi E., Hathaway, Sandee. *What to Expect the Toddler Years.* (Workman, 1994)

Gree, Christopher, MD. *Toddler Taming.* (Ballantine, 1985)

Jordan, Timothy J., MD. *Food Fights and Bedtime Battles: A Working Parent's Guide to Negotiating Daily Power Struggles.* (Berkeley, 2001)

Karp, Harvey. *The Happiest Toddler on the Block: The New Way to Stop the Daily Battle of Wills and Raise a Secure and Well-Behaved One- to Four-Year-Old.* (Bantam Doubleday Dell Publishing Group, 2004)

Kelly, Jeffrey, MD. *Solving Your Child's Behavior Problems, An Everyday Guide for Parents.* (Little, Brown, 1983)

Kurcinka, Mary S. *Raising Your Spirited Child: A Guide for Parents Whose Child Is More Intense, Sensitive, Perceptive, Persistent, Energetic.* (HarperCollins, 1991)

Kurcinka, Mary Sheedy. *Kids, Parents, and Power Struggles: Winning for a Lifetime.* (HarperCollins, 2001)

Laforge, Ann E. *Tantrums: Secrets to Calming the Storm.* (Simon & Schuster, 1996)

Margulis, Jennifer (Editor). *Toddler: Real-life Stories of Those Fickle, Irrational, Urgent, Tiny People We Love.* (Seal Press, 2003).

Mitchell, Grace, Dewsnap, Lois. *Help! What Do I Do About . . . ? . . . Biting, Tantrums, and 47 Other Everyday Problems.* (Scholastic, 1994)

Mountrose, Phillip. *Getting Thru to Kids: Problem Solving with Children Ages 6 to 18.* (Holistic Communications, 1991)

Nelsen, Jane, Ed.D, Erwin, Cheryl, Duffy, Roslyn. *Positive Discipline: The First Three Years: From Infant to Toddler—Laying the Foundation for Raising a Capable, Confident Child.* (Crown, 1998)

Neugebauer, Bonnie (Editor). *Alike and Different: Exploring Our Humanity with Young Children.* (Exchange Press, 1992)

Pruett, Kyle D. *Me, Myself and I: How Children Build Their Sense of Self: 18 to 36 Months.* (Goddard Press, 1999)

Remboldt, Carole. *Helping Kids Resolve Conflicts Without Violence* (Johnson Institute Resources for Parents). (Johnson Institute, 1996)

Rosemond, John K. *Making the "Terrible" Two's Terrific!* (Andrews McMeel, 1993)

Sears, William, Sears, Martha. *The Discipline Book.* (Little, Brown, 1997)

Shure, Myrna B. *Raising a Thinking Child: Help Your Young Child to Resolve Everyday Conflicts and Get Along with Others (The "I Can Problem Solve" Program).* (Picket Books, 1996)

Stern, Daniel. *The First Relationship: Infants and Mother.* (Harvard University Press, 1977)

Thomas, A., Chess, S. *Temperament and Development.* (Brunner/ Mazel, 1977)

Turecki, Stanley, MD, Turner, Leslie. *The Difficult Child.* (Bantam, 1989)

Warwick, Pudney, Whitehouse, Eliane. *A Volcano in My Tummy: Helping Children to Handle Anger: A Resources Book for Parents, Caregivers and Teachers.* (Now Society Publishers, 1996)

White, Burton L. *Raising a Happy, Unspoiled Child.* (Simon & Schuster, 1994)

Williamson, P. *Good Kids, Bad Behavior: Helping Children Learn Self-Discipline.* (Simon & Schuster, 1990)

Web Sites for Parents

DrGreene.com
Dr. Greene answers questions about behavior development and more. Browse through his articles or join him in a scheduled chat.
www.drgreene.com

AskDrSears.com
On this Web site, you will find information about feeding and sleep problems and childhood illnesses, along with sound parenting advice.
www.askdrsears.com

PositiveDiscipline.com
This is the place for tons of resources, book excepts, and articles.
www.positivediscipline.com

KidsHealth
KidsHealth has separate areas for kids, teens, and parents.
www.kidshealth.org

Babycenter.com
A huge site! You will find tools, articles, an online store, chats, and a message board.
www.babycenter.com

Parenthood.com
This site has information on development through the life span.
www.parenthood.com

Parenting: Babies & Toddlers
Check out the tons of links, articles, and discussion board.
http://babyparenting.about.com

A Child's Development Calendar
Read all about your child and her accomplishments at each stage of development.
www.vtnea.org/vtnea14.htm

The National Parenting Center
This wonderful site includes articles from many experts and also includes product recall information.
www.tnpc.com

PositiveParenting.com
A huge site with its own bookstore and newsletter.
www.positiveparenting.com

Amazingmoms.com
You can spend a week on this site exploring all the tips, recipes, and articles about child development and family life.
www.amazingmoms.com

FamilyFun.com
Ideas and advice for potty training, discipline, and development. You will also find lots of fun activity ideas, too.
www.familyfun.go.com/parenting/

National Childbirth Trust
Tells you everything you need to know about babies and children, from conception to growing up.
www.nct.org.uk

Kids Health
Lively, informative web site with advice on a full range of toddler and child behaviour problems and solutions.
www.kidshealth.org

Royal College of Psychiatrists
Follow the links to 'Mental health and growing up' for the official

psychiatric view of tantrums and their causes, and for links to local psychiatrists.

www.rcpsych.ac.uk

Tiny Tums

Sponsored by Heinz baby foods, this has an interactive Frequently Asked Questions link under 'Toddlers', which you can use to ask about your specific problems.

www.tinytums.co.uk

Baby Centre

This is a UK version of the American Baby Center site, offering the same features and online messages.

www.babycentre.co.uk

Practical Parenting

The online version of the popular magazine is full of advice and links to related topics.

www.practicalparent.org.uk

Good News Family Care

This Christian web site offers sound practical information on toddler development and and advice on coping with tantrums.

www.gnfc.org.uk

BBC.co.uk

Follow the link to 'Your kids' for advice and discussion on behaviour issues; easy links to a full selection of CBeebies programmes and other BBC products for children.

www.bbc.co.uk/parenting

Children First

The NHS web site has specific links to 'Child development', 'Toddler' and 'Tantrum', and can also be used to locate NHS child behaviourists and support services quickly and easily.

www.childrenfirst.nhs.uk

Peep
Advice and support from this bright, helpful web site.
www.peep.org.uk

Parentline Plus
Down-to-earth, practical help for a whole range of toddler problems.
www.parentlineplus.org.uk

Allkids
Online parenting magazine and directory with a great variety of links.
www.allkids.co.uk

Childcare Link
Part of the National Childcare Strategy, this aims to help parents find childcare, and has links to other government child initiatives.
www.childcare.gov.uk

One Parent Families
Specific advice and links to other sites for single parents.
www.oneparentfamilies.co.uk

Glossary

adaptability: The ability to adapt or change one's behavior in response to the environment.

adolescence: The teenage years, typically between twelve and eighteen years of age.

aggression: Behavior that inflicts physical or emotional harm on someone or something else.

ambivalent attachment: The lack of a secure bond with the caregiver that results in the child's becoming lonely, insecure, or withdrawn.

assertiveness: A way of interacting with others that makes sure that your own needs and desires are met without harming anyone.

attachment: A close and secure relationship between a child and his primary caregiver.

Attention Deficit Disorder (ADD): Attention Deficit Disorder (ADD) generally has two main behavioral components: difficulty paying attention and impulsiveness. When a child is also hyperactive, then she is said to have ADHD.

authoritarian: A parenting style where the parent has full control. This style is often harsh and punitive.

authoritative: A parenting style where the parent has most of the control, but children's input and opinions are respected.

autism: Autism is a broad-spectrum developmental disorder.

autonomy: A feeling of independence; the ability to make independent choices and take independent action.

behavior modification: Attempting to change or modify a child's behavior by the controlled use of tokens or rewards to reinforce positive behavior.

bipolar disorder: Bipolar disorder, sometimes also called manic depression, is identified in children who exhibit extreme and sometimes rapid changes in mood, energy, thinking, or behavior.

bonding: The process of forming an attachment or relationship between two people.

cognitive development: Refers to the development of mental or intellectual processes. Cognitive development includes language, problem solving, and memory.

collective monologue: A conversation where two or more people are speaking but no one seems to be listening or responding to anyone else.

consequences: The direct result of a behavior. If I do this, then this will happen.

defiance: Willful or intentional opposition.

discipline: To guide or teach someone, usually referring to helping a child learn safe behavior and self-control.

displaced aggression: Aggression that is aimed at someone or something that was not the original cause of anger or frustration.

echolalia: Seen in autistic children, this is when the individual repeatedly echoes back what is said to them.

egocentric: The perception of a young child where he can see the world only through his own eyes and cannot understand anyone else's viewpoint. The egocentric child sees himself as the center of the world.

empathy: The ability to see and understand another person's viewpoint or feelings as if one is experiencing it oneself.

enuresis: Bed-wetting. It is common in children through the age of five.

expressive language: Language used for expression. Speaking and writing are forms of expressive language.

external gestation: A time when you carry your infant close to your body, allowing your child to hear your heartbeat and voice and feel constant closeness and touch.

food jag: A period of time when the child becomes very picky and will eat only one or just a few things.

gratification: Having one's needs or desires met.

hyperactive: To be restless, fidgety, or easily distracted.

"I" messages: A positive statement that directly communicates the speaker's wishes or needs. This statement always starts with the word I. For example, "I wish that you would stop fussing and clean up your room."

imitation: A mode of learning where the child observes a model and the consequences of their actions.

impulsive: The tendency to act without first considering the consequences. To look before you leap.

infant: A child between birth and one year of age.

insecure attachment: A lack of a secure bond with the caregiver that results in the child's being clingy and craving attention or approval.

instrumental aggression: Aggressive behavior that is goal directed, such as pushing someone out of the way so that you can get a seat on the bus.

intrinsic motivation: Motivation or action that is not influenced by external consequences or rewards. To do something because of your conscience.

learned helplessness: The loss of motivation to try out or attempt a new skill or activity, sure that one will only fail anyhow.

model: To provide an example. Someone who is imitated: role model.

motherese: Also know as parentese. Motherese is a universal style of speech that adults unconsciously adopt when they are speaking to infants. Someone who is speaking motherese talks in a high-pitched voice, speaks slowly, and uses repetition and exaggeration of sounds.

motivation: A driving force behind behavior. People are usually motivated to get their needs met.

night terror: A phenomenon that occurs in young children. Unlike nightmares, night terrors occur while the child is in a deep sleep. Although children may scream or cry, they are not fully awake and do not recall the incident when they do awaken.

nurture: To care for someone. Someone who is nurturing is loving, warm, and responsive.

object permanence: The understanding that something or someone still exists even when it cannot be seen or heard.

objective morality: Described by psychologist Jean Piaget, it is the view that your child judges good or bad behavior based on the result of the action rather than the motivation behind it.

oppositional defiant disorder (ODD): This disorder is marked by a persistent pattern of behavior where the child is very negative, hostile, and defiant.

peer group: Other people in your same age range or generation.

permissive: A style of parenting where the parents take very little control. Very few limits are set on children's behavior. Moreover, existing limits are poorly enforced.

preschooler: A child between three and six years of age.

proprioceptive system: Refers to your child's awareness of her body and its location in space.

punishment: A negative response to a child's behavior, designed to stop the behavior. There are three main types of punishment: consequential punishment, verbal punishment, and physical punishment.

receptive language: Language used for receiving information. Listening and reading are forms of receptive language.

redirection: A discipline technique where the child is guided to change his behavior to a more appropriate alternative.

reflective listening: A statement that shows that the listener is aware of the speaker's concerns, feelings, or interests. For example, "I can see that you are very upset, but I need you to clean up your room before you can go outside to play."

reinforcement: The result of an action. A positive consequence to a behavior will increase the likelihood of a child's repeating the behavior in hope that she will achieve the desired result. Conversely, a negative result will increase the likelihood of a child's stopping the behavior to avoid the negative consequence.

scaffolding: When you give your child support and guidance to move on to the next step of skill achievement or complexity.

secure attachment: When a child has a bond with his primary caregiver that allows him to be well adjusted, trusting, secure, and confident.

self-control: The ability to independently recognize, interpret, and display emotion in an appropriate fashion.

self-injurious behavior: A child's deliberately hurting herself without intending to commit suicide. Common self-injurious behaviors include cutting, burning, and biting.

self-stimulation: Repetitive physical actions such as rocking, spinning, and head banging. Sometimes self-stimulation behaviors are a sign of stress or autism.

sensory integration disorder (SID): A child with SID has insufficient neurological processing of sensory information. He may be over- or under-sensitive to different types of sensory information, and he may often misinterpret mild sensory signals to perceive them as causing great discomfort.

separation anxiety: The display of anxious behavior when a child is being separated from someone with whom she has formed an attachment. This may occur anywhere from ten months to four years of age.

stranger anxiety: A display of anxious behavior that an infant will show toward someone when he begins to realize that she is not his mother or primary caregiver. This behavior usually peaks between nine and twelve months of age.

tactile system: The sensory system that guides how we perceive light touch, pressure, pain, or temperature.

temper tantrum: A temper tantrum is essentially an uncontrolled outburst of emotion. Temper tantrums are sometimes referred to as fits or melt-downs and are a common behavior during childhood.

temperament: Temperament is your child's inborn disposition. Your child's temperament is his characteristic way of responding and reacting to events and his environment.

toddler: A child between the ages of one and three years.

token: An object or mark that represents a reward. Tokens such as stickers or poker chips are often used as part of a reward system.

transitional object: Any object that a child uses as a security object to help her cope with separation anxiety. The object often symbolizes a tie to home, mother, or security. Common transitional objects include blankets and teddy bears.

vestibular system: This system has to do with the inner ear, affecting the child's sense of balance and her ability to detect her own movement.